ERASMUS STRIBLING, AGED 62
Æ 25

The

STRIBLING FAMILY
OF VIRGINIA:

A GENEALOGY

Excerpted from:

Some Virginia Families, Being Genealogies of the Kinney, Stribling,
Trout, McIlhany, Milton, Rogers, Tate, Snickers, Taylor,
McCormick, and Other Families of Virginia.

Staunton, Virginia: 1903

By

HUGH MILTON MCILHANY, JR. M. A., Ph. D.

Notice

In many older books, foxing (or discoloration) occurs and, in some instances, print lightens with wear and age. Reprinted books, such as this, often duplicate these flaws, notwithstanding efforts to reduce or eliminate them. The pages of this reprint have been digitally enhanced and, where possible, the flaws eliminated in order to provide clarity of content and a pleasant reading experience.

The Stribling Family of Virginia: A Genealogy

Excerpted from:

Some Virginia Families, Being Genealogies of the Kinney, Stribling, Trout, McIlhany, Milton, Rogers, Tate, Snickers, Taylor, McCormick, and Other Families of Virginia.

Originally published
Staunton, Virginia
1903

Reprinted by:

Janaway Publishing, Inc.
732 Kelsey Ct.
Santa Maria, California 93454
(805) 925-1038
www.janawaygenealogy.com

2012

ISBN: 978-1-59641-294-1

Made in the United States of America

Publisher's Preface

This work has been excerpted from the book, *Some Virginia Families, Being Genealogies of the Kinney, Stribling, Trout, McIlhany, Milton, Rogers, Tate, Snickers, Taylor, McCormick, and Other Families of Virginia*, by Hugh Milton McIlhany, Jr., which was originally published in Staunton, Virginia, in 1903, and includes pages 31 to 111 of the original volume. This work retains those original page numbers.

Janaway Publishing, Inc.

THE STRIBLING FAMILY.

§ 22. There is a tradition preserved among some of the Striblings of Tennessee to the effect that this family is of Polish origin, the name having been originally spelled Striblinski, and that Thomas Stribling, the first of the name in this country, and said to have been closely related to one of the kings of Poland, was exiled from his native land because of his political or religious views or both. While I have been unable to find any historical basis for such a theory, the plausibility of the Polish origin of the name is borne out by the recurrence of the names Sigismund and Casimir in the different branches of the family. I am inclined to believe, however, that even if the name had such an origin, there must have been a sojourn of a generation or two in England before the emigration of the family to this country. There are Striblings residing in England today whose ancestors lived in Devonshire; and at the very time that Thomas Stribling settled in Virginia, one Benjamin Stribling with his family resided at Lavenham, Suffolk, England.

THOMAS STRIBLING probably came to America about the year 1710, and settled in Stafford County, Virginia. On July 11, 1727 there was granted to "Thomas Striblin of Stafford County" 1050 acres "on the middle grounds twixt Broad Run of Occaquan and Bull Run", which property was in that part of Stafford which shortly afterwards became Prince William County. Here he resided, in Dettinger Parish, about twenty years, when he removed to Frederick County. In 1752 "Thomas Stribling of Prince William, Gent." purchased 600 acres of land near Winchester. He died in 1755, his will being recorded March 25, 1755 in Prince William County, his sons Francis and Taliaferro qualifying as executors; but the will book was lost or destroyed during the Civil War. His estate in Frederick County was appraised May 3, 1755, and that in Prince William May 26, 1755. Shortly after 1715 he married *Elizabeth Taliaferro*, daughter of John Taliaferro of Essex, who represented that County in the House of Burgesses in 1699 (see §87). On account of the loss of his will, the names of all his children cannot be given with certainty. The three oldest are named in the will of Robert Taliaferro of Essex (dated Dec. 3, 1725; approved June 21, 1726), who mentions his sister Elizabeth, the wife of "Thomas Stripling", and her sons Francis, William, and Taliaferro "Stripling". Francis Stribling and Dorothy his wife were living in Prince William County in 1775. He inherited part of his father's estate in that County, but nothing further is known of him   William Stribling moved to Frederick County, and died there unmarried(?) in 1748, his father qualifying as his executor Feb. 7, 1748-9. Taliaferro Stribling also settled in Frederick County, as shown below

That there were other children of Thomas and Elizabeth Stribling besides these three cannot be doubted. Thomas Stribling, the progenitor of the South Carolina branch of the family, was surely one of them (see §72). On July 23, 1754 one Colclough Stribling was paid for traveling 45 miles to and from the Prince William Court as a witness. On Feb 7, 1744 a tract of 119 acres was granted to Benjamin Stribling of Prince William County. A Samuel Stripling, aged thirty-three, enlisted in Caroline County in Capt. Mercer's Company on Dec 4, 1754, to fight the Indians. These must have been sons either of Thomas Stribling or of a brother who came to this country with him. That there was such a brother is indicated by the inventory of a William Stribling, deceased, recorded in Stafford County in 1765, the said William being either a brother or nephew of the first Thomas. I am convinced that Capt. Sigismund Stribling of the Revolutionary Army was a son of this Thomas. He is called "Uncle Sigismund" in several letters of the grand-children of Taliaferro Stribling, but could hardly have been the latter's son, as will be shown below. He was very old at the time of his death at "Hopewell" in 1816, having been born hardly later than 1740. He was a bachelor, and left his property to his name-sake, Sigismund Stribling, son of Francis Stribling, §45. Heitman's "Historical Register" of the Officers of the Continental Army gives the following record of his service: "2nd lieut 12th Va , Dec. 1776; 1st lieut, 10th May, 1777; regiment designated 8th Va., 14th Sep, 1778; Capt. —1781, and served to——". The Revolutionary Records in the State Land Office show that on June 21, 1783, 4666⅔ acres of land were granted to Capt. Sigismund Stribling for seven years service. On Oct. 23, 1807, 833 acres additional were granted to "Capt. Segismond Stribling as Captain of the Continental line for one year and three months service more than seven years". There is also a warrant for 400 acres, Oct 22, 1784, to William Stribling as Sergeant of the Continental Line, who enlisted for the war and served through. This was doubtless the same William Stribling who was pensioned in Fauquier County in 1818 for Revolutionary Service. There was a Benjamin Stribling, who, with his wife, Ann Vawters, and several children (Thomas T., George, Willis, and others), moved from Fauquier County, Va., to Scott County, Kentucky, about 1795, and who has left numerous descendants in Tennessee, Indiana and other western states. This Benjamin and the last mentioned William were evidently brothers, and perhaps sons of Francis or Benjamin Stribling, sons of the original Thomas Stribling.

§ 23.   **Taliaferro Stribling,** son of Thomas and Elizabeth Taliaferro Stribling, was born in Stafford County about 1723. In early manhood he moved with his father to Frederick County, and at the latter's death inherited the 600 acre plantation referred to above. This he "and Elizabeth his wife" sold Nov. 7, 1771, the deed stating that the property had been willed to him by his father Thomas Stribling. On Oct. 16, 1771 he purchased the estate called "Hopewell", which descended to his son Francis. His will, made Oct. 4, 1774, was recorded in the Frederick court Dec. 7, 1774. His personal estate, including 30 negroes, was appraised April 24, 1775 at £1569. I have not been able to determine accurately the maiden name of his wife Elizabeth. The uniform tradition in the family has been that this Stribling, name unknown, married a Mary Taliaferro of Gloucester County, sister of the Elizabeth Taliaferro who married Edward Snickers of Frederick (see § 91). This could not have been the case. The fact that his own name was Taliaferro and that his mother was Elizabeth Taliaferro is sufficient ground for the tradition. And his wife was certainly named Elizabeth, as shown by the deed referred to above. I conjecture that her name was *Elizabeth Wright*, for the following reasons. Two of their grand-children, *Elizabeth* Stribling *Wright* Milton and Dr. Matthew *Wright* Stribling, bore that name, and I know of no other source from which it could have come. Then there is on record in Prince William County, dated March 29, 1742, the will of one Francis Wright, son of John Wright of that County, mentioning his wife *Anne*, and three young daughters, names not given. *Sigismund* Massey of Stafford County, probably a relative of the Striblings, was executor of the will. A short while after the death of Francis Wright, Thomas Stribling, Sr., was appointed guardian of these children. If Taliaferro Stribling had, about 1755, married one of these daughters, named Elizabeth, with whom he must have been well acquainted, all the facts in the case would be explained, as well as the origin of the name of his only daughter *Anne* Milton.

Taliaferro and Elizabeth Stribling had at least six children. In his will he leaves to his son Francis Stribling "the land whereon I live on condition he pay my son Taliaferro 100£ as soon as he become 21 years of age". After the payment of his just debts, the rest of his estate was to be divided equally among "my six children—Francis, Taliaferro, Ann, Thomas, William and John". From the wording of this will I conclude that Francis, at that time only eighteen years of age, was the oldest child; that Taliaferro was the second; that the other children are named in the order of their ages, this fact being supported by the dates of their marriages and other points to be mentioned later; that they were all, therefore, under age at the time; that those six were all of his children; and that his wife had died between the years 1771 and 1774, as she is not mentioned in the will. This of course excludes Capt. Sigismund Stribling (see §22) from the number of his children, and shows that they were brothers. He died Oct. 5, 1774, and was buried at "Hopewell". The following are his descendants:

----

§24 A.   FRANCIS STRIBLING, b. Frederick County, in 1756; d. "Hopewell", Sep. 6, 1823, "aged 67"; m. "Belvidere", near Charlestown, W. Va., in 1783, *Nancy Tate* (b. ib. Feb. 15, 1763; d. "Hopewell", July 4, 1825; for her ancestry

ERASMUS STRIBLING, AGED 21
Æ 25

see §88); they were both interred at "Hopewell". He inherited this estate from his father, and lived there all his life, by his industry and thrift accumulating a great amount of property. Here all of his ten children were born, and to them he gave the best education available. He was a man of lasting influence in the community, being especially interested in the public charities of the county. At the time of his death his personal property was valued at $8000.00, while his landed possessions were very large. In his will, made June 4, 1823 and approved Oct. 6. 1823, he mentions his children,—Erasmus, Taliaferro, Francis, Magnus T., Thomas, George W., Nancy Neill, and Margaret P. Pennybacker; the children of his daughter Mary T. Crawford, deceased; and the daughter and only child of his son Sigismund, deceased. The "Hopewell" estate he left to his wife Nancy, to be sold at her death and equally divided among his children. Accordingly in 1826 it was sold to Fayette Washington, and the name was changed to "Waverly". His son Dr. Taliaferro Stribling qualified as executor of his will on a bond of $70,000.00.

§25 I. ERASMUS STRIBLING, b. "Hopewell", June 1, 1784; d. at the residence of his son-in-law, John S Lewis, in Mason Co., W. Va., July 2, 1858; m. Staunton, April 23, 1807, *Matilda Kinney;* see KINNEY FAMILY, §3.

A notice written at the time of his death, says in part of Mr. Stribling,—"Endowed in a remarkable degree with all those mental and social qualities which fit a man for usefulness and endear him to society, it was his privilege during his long life to fill many honorable and important stations". He studied at Washington College, Lexington, Va., during the sessions of 1800–1803. While he was at an early date a merchant in Staunton, by profession he was a lawyer. The well known Stribling Springs property was owned and developed by him, from whom it derived its name. In early life he was for several years Clerk of the old District Court of the Sweet Springs. On Aug. 29, 1812 he was elected Clerk of the County Court of Augusta (to which county he had removed in 1805), and held that office till July, 1831. In 1846 he was appointed Clerk of the U. S. Court for the Western District of Virginia, which office he resigned in 1857, because of his advanced age and infirmity. Besides these positions he was, at different times, a Justice of the Peace for the County of Augusta, Clerk of the Corporation Court, Recorder of the town of Staunton in 1814, '15 and '17, and Mayor in 1816 and '18. On July 21, 1812 he was commissioned Captain of a company of Artillery of the Virginia militia, but was never called upon for active service. In 1816 he served with General Robert Porterfield and General John Brown as Commissioner of Elections for his district. "It may be said with perfect truth that all the trusts confided to him were discharged with fidelity, industry and unusual ability. His social qualities were of the very first order. Hospitable, sympathetic and well informed, it was impossible for any one to know him and not to love him. In the days of his prosperity his hospitable board was the great centre of attraction for all; and the charms of his conversation, the freedom of his entertainments, and his well known benevolence of disposition, made his house the resort of fashion as well as the shelter of the distressed. For many years before his death, the cloud of an adverse fortune and the death of a beloved wife, had closed his hospitable door, and dispersed his large and interesting family. But still he was cheerful—still beloved, and in his latter years he exhibited what he had no opportunity of exhibiting before: that noble, manly nature, which enabled him to withstand the shock of adversity." In the same strain Judge Sheffey writes in the "Memorials of Virginia Clerks": "He was a man of rare intelligence and geniality of nature, a fine talker, and warm hearted and devoted in his friendships. During the time, at least the earlier part of the time, he held the office of County Clerk, he was one of the foremost men of the county in wealth, prosperity, possessions and influence, and no one was more cordially beloved by all in the community than he. His heart was filled with gentle, almost womanly, affections, and he scattered his favors and kindnesses around him with a lavish hand."

When the Episcopal congregation was permanently organized at Staunton in 1820, Mr. Stribling was amongst the foremost with his efforts and with his purse, and was a member of the first vestry elected. While in early life he had been somewhat dissipated and careless concerning religion, for many years preceding his death he was a most worthy and exemplary member of the Church. When it was impossible for his family to attend worship Sunday mornings at the church in town, it was always his custom to have the service and a sermon read for them and their servants at "Oak Hill", their country home. Of his 140 descendants, only eleven living bear the name of Stribling.

Mrs. Stribling was a woman of unusual attractiveness. Several pictures are extant which were painted by her at the age of sixteen. She died in the very prime of life, leaving a family of eleven children, as follows:

§26   1. Jacob Kinney Stribling, b. Staunton, Feb. 10, 1808; d. Parkersburg, W. Va., Sep. 10, 1854; m. Frederick City, Md., Aug. 21, 1840, *Harriett Engleman* (b. Augusta County, about 1822; d. Staunton, Nov. 4, 1886); he was at one time deputy clerk of the Augusta County Court.

    (1). Peter Engleman Stribling, b. Staunton, July 12, 1842; d. Giles Court House, Va., June 17, 1864, of a wound received in the War.

    (2). Erasmus Stribling, b. Staunton, Jan. 10, 1844; d. Newport News, Feb. 1, 1898: m. Chesterfield County, Va., Dec. 19, 1872, *Mary Ann Talley* (b. ib. July 28, 1850; 1. Richmond).

      a. Charles Alford Stribling, b. Petersburg, Sep. 11, 1873; d. ib. Sep. 16, 1873.

      b. Eva Stribling, b. ib. Sep. 28, 1874; m. Washington, D. C., Aug. 10, 1891, *Charles Francis Hubbard* (b. Brooklyn, N. Y., April 17, 1871; he is a grocer); 1. Richmond.

        (a). Annie Mary Hubbard, b. Richmond, Sep. 5, 1893; d. ib. Aug. 10, 1895.

        (b). Thomas Francis Hubbard, b. ib. Jan. 22, 1898.

      c. Erasmus Stribling, b. Norfolk, March 30, 1877; 1. Richmond.

      d. Bettie Ann Kinney Stribling, b. Tarboro, N. C., March 4, 1880; d. Richmond, June 18, 1881.

   e. CHESLEY KINNEY STRIBLING, b. ib June 30, 1882; 1. ib.

(3). SALLIE ANN STRIBLING, b. Staunton, July 29, 1845; m. Point Pleasant, W. Va., Nov. 5, 1867, *Andrew Joseph McMullin* (b. ib. Aug. 13, 1840; he is a tobacco manufacturer); 1. Sebree, Webster Co., Ky.

   a. HATTIE LEWIS MCMULLIN, b. McMullin's Landing, Ky., Aug. 27, 1869; m. Sebree, Ky., March 18, 1891, *Joseph Samuel Montague* (b. Cromwell, Ohio Co., Ky., Dec. 18, 1864; he is a merchant); 1. Delaware, Ky.

     (a). ETTA NORINE MONTAGUE, b. Sebree, Ky., Feb. 27, 1892.

     (b). SARAH MONTAGUE, b. ib. July 22, 1894.

     (c). MARY ELLEN MONTAGUE, b. ib. March 28, 1896; d. ib. Dec. 18, 1896.

     (d). JOSEPHINE MONTAGUE, b. ib. July 14, 1900.

   b. NORA ALLEN MCMULLIN, b. Delaware, Ky., March 23, 1871; m. Dixon, Ky., Sep. 7, 1893, *John Thornton Riddle* (b. Petersburg, Oct. 1871; d. Sebree, Ky., Sep 8, 1893); 1. ib.

     (a). MARY THORNTON RIDDLE, b. ib. June 4, 1894.

   c. FANNIE BURBANK MCMULLIN, b. Livermore, Ky., Feb. 4, 1874; d. Henderson, Ky., Sep. 6, 1888.

   d. SALLIE LYNN MCMULLIN, b. Livermore, Ky., Dec. 31, 1876; m. Sebree, Ky., Jan. 12, 1899, *Frank Marion Edwards* (b. ib. July 26, 1875; he is a farmer); 1. ib.

     (a). CHARLES LAMBERT EDWARDS, b. ib. Dec. 10, 1899.

     (b). JAMES MCMULLIN EDWARDS, b. ib. July 28, 1901.

DR. FRANCIS TALIAFERRO STRIBLING
Æ 27

      e. JOSEPH MCMULLIN, b. Livermore, Ky.,
Dec. 25, 1878; d. ib. Jan. 14, 1879.

      f. NANNIE BRANSON MCMULLIN, b. Henderson, Ky., Jan. 20, 1880; 1. Sebree, Ky.

      g. STEWART NELSON MCMULLIN, b. Henderson, Ky., Feb. 22, 1883; is in the U. S.
Army in the Philippines.

      h. KATIE HAYDEN MCMULLIN, b. Sebree,
Ky., Jan. 8, 1885; d. ib. Nov. 20, 1885.

      i. AGNES SEHON MCMULLIN, b. ib. June
29, 1886; 1. ib.

§27   (4). ELIZABETH ANN KINNEY STRIBLING, b.
Staunton, April 10, 1851; d. Richmond, April 11,
1895; m. McKinney, Tex., Dec. 3, 1872, *Richard
Dangerfield Ryan*, her third cousin; see §100.

      (5). JOHN WAYT STRIBLING, b. Staunton, July
2, 1854; 1. Gypsum, Texas.

2. FRANCIS TALIAFERRO STRIBLING, b. Staunton,
Jan. 20, 1810; d. ib. July 23, 1874; m. near Staunton,
May 17, 1832, *Henrietta Frances Cuthbert* (b. Norfolk,
July 3, 1813; d. Staunton, Feb. 28, 1889); he graduated at the University of Virginia in 1829; he was
one of the most distinguished physicians of his time,
and was for many years the Superintendent of the
Western State Hospital at Staunton.

      (1). ELLA MATILDA STRIBLING, b. Staunton,
March 5, 1833; d. ib. June 28, 1885; m. ib. June
5, 1867, *Hugh Lee Powell* (b. Leesburg, July 20,
1839; he married a second time and is living at
Leesburg).

      a. LUCY LEE POWELL, b. Staunton, Feb. 5,
1868; 1. ib.

      b. LOUISE MATHILDE POWELL, b. ib. March
12, 1871; 1. Richmond.

      c. FRANCIS TALIAFERRO STRIBLING POWELL,
b. Staunton, April 13, 1874; 1. New York City.

      (2). FANNIE CUTHBERT STRIBLING, b. Staunton,
Dec. 8, 1836; m. ib. Feb. 8, 1860, *Richard Taylor
Foster* (b. Petersburg, Sep. 14, 1830; d. Richmond, April 27, 1875); 1. Staunton.

a. HENRIETTA CUTHBERT FOSTER, b. ib.; 1. Philadelphia.

b. MARY ENDERS FOSTER, b. Richmond; 1. Staunton.

c. RICHARD TAYLOR FOSTER (1st), b. Richmond, June 30, 1863; d. ib. July 14, 1863.

d. FRANK STRIBLING FOSTER, b. Goochland County, July 13, 1864; is connected with the First National Bank, Birmingham, Ala.

e. RICHARD TAYLOR FOSTER (2nd), b. Richmond, June 24, 1865; d. Staunton, Aug. 31, 1865.

f. ARTHUR PEGRAM FOSTER, b. ib. Oct. 27, 1866; d. ib. Sep. 28, 1891.

(3). FRANCIS TALIAFERRO STRIBLING, b. ib. Aug. 13, 1845; m. Norfolk, April 23, 1889, *Olive Caldwell Jackson* (b. Leesburg, July 22, 1857); 1. Staunton.

(4). HENRIETTA BERKELEY STRIBLING, b. Staunton, Sep. 17, 1852; d. ib. Aug. 6, 1893.

§28 3. NANCY STRIBLING, b. ib. Oct. 8, 1811; d. Washington, D. C., Jan. 4, 1882; m. Staunton, July 31, 1828, *John C. Bowyer* (b. ib. Oct. 4, 1803; d. ib. May 31, 1880; he studied law, but afterward turned his attention to journalism, editing papers in Winchester and Alexandria; after the War he held a government position in Washington.

(1). MATILDA KINNEY STRIBLING BOWYER, b. Staunton, June 8, 1829; d. Washington, D. C., Sep. 26, 1853; m. Staunton, Oct. 23, 1850, *Lieut. Pierce Crosby* (b. Chester, Pa., Jan. 16, 1824; d. Washington, D. C., June 16, 1899; he was married four times, and at the time of his death was Admiral in the U. S. Navy).

(2). ELIZABETH LEWIS BOWYER, b. Rockbridge County, June 2, 1831; d. Winchester, July 22, 1892; m. Washington, D. C., Oct. 5, 1854, *Dr. David Porter Heap* (b. Marseilles, France, in 1828; d. Germantown, Pa., Aug. 11, 1866; he was in the U. S. Diplomatic Service).

a. ANNIE ELLEN HEAP, b. Tunis, Africa,
June 19, 1855; d. Washington, D. C., Feb.
11, 1889; m. ib. July 5, 1877, *Reginald Fairfax Nicolson* (b. ib. Dec. 15, 1852; he is a
Lieutenant Commander in the U. S. Navy).

   (a). MARY JONES NICOLSON, b. Washington, D. C., June 13, 1878; 1. ib.

   (b). REGINALD FAIRFAX NICOLSON, b.
   ib. Dec. 18, 1879; d. Winchester, July
   2, 1890.

b. SAMUEL LAWRENCE HEAP, b. Tunis,
Africa, Dec. 22, 1856; is a Paymaster in the
U. S. Navy.

c. MARGARET MATILDA HEAP, b. Tunis,
Africa, April 6, 1859; m. Washington, D. C.,
Jan. 20, 1892, *John Spotswood Garland* (b. ib.
Feb. 15, 1859; he is a civil engineer in the
office of the District Commissioners); 1. ib.

   (a). ELIZABETH BOWYER GARLAND, b.
   ib. Dec. 20, 1892.

   (b). JOHN SPOTSWOOD GARLAND, b.
   Georgetown, D. C., Dec. 25, 1895.

   (c). MARY TRUXTUN GARLAND, b. Washington, D. C., June 19, 1897.

d. EVELINA MARY HEAP, b. Louisville, Ky.,
April 25, 1863; m. Washington, D. C., June
12, 1889, *Albert Gleaves* (b. Nashville, Tenn.,
Jan. 1, 1858; he is a Lieutenant Commander
in the U. S. Navy); 1. Washington, D. C.

   (a). ANNIE HEAP GLEAVES, b. ib. July
   15, 1890.

   (b). EVELINA PORTER GLEAVES, b. ib.
   May 26, 1895.

(3). HENRY MORTON BOWYER, b. Rockbridge
County, April 28, 1833; d. ib. April 4, 1839.

(4). FANNIE MORTON BOWYER, b. ib. June 23,
1835; d. ib. Nov. 3, 1842.

(5). CHARLOTTE AUGUSTA BOWYER, b. ib. Oct.
27, 1838; d. Alexandria, June 5, 1853.

(6). Infant, b. and d. Rockbridge County, July 17, 1840.

(7) ALICE STUART BOWYER, b. Winchester, Dec. 23, 1845; d. Washington, D. C., May 13, 1859.

4. ERASMUS STRIBLING, b. Staunton, Aug. 4, 1813; d. ib. Sep. 20, 1828.

§29   5. MARY TATE STRIBLIŃG, b. ib. Feb. 10, 1815; d. Mason County, W. Va , April 22, 1887; m. Staunton, Aug. 30, 1838, *John Stuart Lewis* (b. Mason Co. W. Va., June 21, 1813; d. Point Pleasant, W. Va., April 13, 1902; p. Col. Andrew Lewis and Margaret Stuart; gr. p. Col. Charles Lewis, killed at the battle of Point Pleasant, and Sarah Murray—Col. John Stuart and Agatha Lewis).

(1). FANNIE LEWIS, b. ib. Nov. 10, 1839; m. ib. May 5, 1862, *John Warth English* (b. Jackson County, W. Va., Jan. 31, 1831; he is a lawyer, and Judge of the Supreme Court of W. Va.); 1. Point Pleasant, W. Va.

    a. LEWIS SEHON ENGLISH, b. ib. May 25, 1864; m. ib. June 5, 1887, *Virginia Hoover* (b. near ib. Feb. 14, 1865); he is a clerk with the Ohio River Ry., at Parkersburg, W. Va.

       (a). EUGENE ENGLISH, b. Point Pleasant, W. Va., Nov. 27, 1889.

    b. MARY STUART ENGLISH, b. ib. March 25, 1867; m. ib. April 26, 1887, *Edward Francis Recktenwald* (b. Logan, Ohio, Nov. 12, 1864; he is in the U. S. Postal Service); 1. Charleston, W. Va.

       (a). FREDERICK LAWRENCE RECKTEN-WALD, b. Point Pleasant, W. Va., Jan. 26, 1888.

       (b). LEWIS RICHARD RECKTENWALD, b. ib. Oct. 11, 1890.

       (c). FRANCIS ENGLISH RECKTENWALD, b. Charleston, W. Va., Jan. 28, 1897.

       (d). MARY MARGUERITE RECKTENWALD, b. ib. Aug. 28, 1900.

   c. MARGARET LYNN ENGLISH, b. Point
Pleasant, W. Va., April 28, 1869; m. ib.
June 15, 1889, *Dr. Lewis VanGilder Guthrie*
(b. ib. Jan. 8, 1868; he is the Physician in
charge of the Hospital for the Insane at
Spencer, W. Va).

      (a). KATHLEEN LEWIS GUTHRIE. b.
Point Pleasant, W. Va., May 5, 1891.

   d. JOHN WARTH ENGLISH, b. ib. Feb. 16,
1874; he is a physician at Bramwell, W. Va.

   e. FANNIE ENGLISH, b. Point Pleasant, W.
Va., Dec. 23, 1874; d. ib. Sep. 23, 1881.

   f. FREDERICK LEE ENGLISH, b. ib. April 17,
1876; d. ib. July 31, 1876.

   g. JULIA WARTH ENGLISH, b. ib. July 31,
1878; d. ib. Oct. 7, 1881.

   h. EUNICE ENGLISH, b. ib. May 4, 1881; m.
ib. Oct. 30, 1901, *Kossuth Tinker McKinstry*
(b. Albany, Ohio, July 8. 1878; he is a merchant); l. Point Pleasant, W. Va.

(2). SARAH ELIZABETH LEWIS, b. ib. Nov. 21,
1841; l. ib.

(3). MATILDA LEWIS, b. ib. April 7, 1844; d.
Staunton, Aug. 29, 1845.

(4). AGNES STUART LEWIS, b. Point Pleasant,
W. Va., June 13, 1846; m. ib. June 14, 1876,
Columbus Sehon (b. Mason County, W. Va., May
3, 1841); l. Huntington, W. Va.

   a. JOHN STUART SEHON, b. Point Pleasant,
W. Va., Oct. 28, 1878; d. Columbus, Ohio,
Jan. 21, 1897.

   b. ANNIE CAMDEN SEHON, b. Point Pleasant, W. Va., Feb. 28, 1882.

(5). MARGARET LYNN LEWIS, b. ib. July 18, 1850;
d. ib. Feb. 22, 1885.

§30 6. MATILDA KINNEY STRIBLING, b. Staunton, Nov.
28, 1816; d. ib. Nov. 2, 1892; m. ib. June 8, 1843,
Nicholas Kinney Trout, her second cousin; see TROUT
FAMILY, §101.

7. SARAH ANN STRIBLING, b. ib. Dec. 3, 1817; d. ib. April 8, 1841.

§31   8. MARGARET FRANCES STRIBLING, b. ib. Sep. 2, 1819; d. "Smithfield", Clarke County, Nov. 22, 1860; m. Staunton, Oct. 31, 1839, *William Dickerson Smith* (b. "Smithfield", June 21, 1815; d. ib. March 19, 1894; see §92).

9. HARRIOT MILTON STRIBLING, b. Staunton, April 20, 1821; d. ib. Nov. 27, 1870.

10. WILLIAM MAGNUS STRIBLING, b. ib. Dec. 7, 1822; d. Dayton, Ohio, April 24, 1902; m. Circleville, Ohio, Sep. 5, 1844, *Anna Maria Crouse* (b. ib. Jan 8, 1826; d. ib. Oct. 30, 1891); he was an M. D. graduate of the University of Pennsylvania in 1843, practiced medicine some years, and was afterwards a farmer.

(1)   FANNIE MATILDA STRIBLING, b. Circleville, Ohio, Dec. 7, 1846; m. ib. Oct. 16, 1867, *Edward Doane Moore* (b. ib. Dec. 20, 1844; d. ib. May 30, 1885; he was a dentist by profession, but never practiced; was President of the City Gas Works); 1. Circleville, Ohio.

    a.   ARCHIBALD STRIBLING MOORE, b. ib. Feb. 21, 1869; d. Eureka, Kansas, Oct. 30, 1872.

    b.   MABEL MOORE, b. Circleville, Ohio, July 4, 1874; m. ib. Jan. 3, 1901, *Percy Ansell Walling* (b. ib. Feb. 14, 1870; he is a lawyer); 1. ib.

    c.   HOWARD BENFORD MOORE, b. ib. Jan. 17, 1876; graduated at the Harvard Law School in June 1902.

(2).   FLORA KINNEY STRIBLING, b. Circleville, Ohio, Sep. 17, 1848; d. ib. April 27, 1857.

(3).   EVANS CROUSE STRIBLING, b. ib. June 19, 1850; d. Mason County, W. Va., Sep. 12, 1851.

(4).   CHARLES ARTHUR STRIBLING, b. Circleville, Ohio, July 29, 1852; m. Columbus, Ohio, Oct. 18, 1876, *Harriette Margaret Williams* (b. ib. Feb. 14, 1856; d. ib. Nov. 7, 1901); he is an architect and a director in the City Deposit Bank); 1. ib.

a. ANNA NAOMI STRIBLING, b. ib. Nov. 5,
1877; m. ib. Feb. 2, 1898, *William Weston
Wood* (b. ib. May 3, 1875; he is in the coal
business); 1. ib.

b. EDWARD WILLIAMS STRIBLING, b. ib.
Nov. 19, 1881; 1. ib.

(5). ERASMUS GRANT STRIBLING, b. Circleville,
Ohio, July 29, 1852; d. ib. May 8, 1857.

(6). JOHN LEWIS STRIBLING, b. ib. July 12, 1857;
m. ib. June 21, 1894, *Emma Alice Hurdle* (b. ib.
Aug. 10, 1863; d. ib. Jan. 18, 1900); he is general manager of the light plant at Circleville, O.

(7). WILLIAM MAGNUS STRIBLING, b. ib. July
11, 1859; d. ib. June 5, 1895.

(8). ROBERT EVANS STRIBLING, b. ib. Jan. 25,
1862; d. ib. April 6, 1874.

§32   11. JOHN WAYT STRIBLING, b. Staunton, April 1–,
1824; d. Orange County, Va., Feb. 17, 1864; m.
Winchester, May 17, 1849, *Anne McCormick*; see
MILTON FAMILY, §179; he was a merchant in Baltimore, Md.

(1). BETTIE TAYLOR STRIBLING, b. Baltimore,
Md., Feb. 14, 1850; d. ib. Feb. 16, 1850.

(2). BUSHROD TAYLOR STRIBLING, b. ib. Sep. 5,
1851; m. Bell County, Texas, Dec. 18, 1890,
Margaret Anna Rich (b. ib. April 26, 1870);
1. Rogers, Bell Co., Texas; he is a farmer.

(3). ALICE MAUDE STRIBLING, b. Winchester,
July 17, 1854; m. Berryville, Sep. 23, 1873, *Randolph Kownslar* (b. ib. July 18, 1850; he is a farmer); 1. Gindale P. O., Bell County, Texas.

a. ALICE MAUDE KOWNSLAR, b. Berryville,
Aug. 14, 1874; d. ib. Dec. 25, 1879.

b. RANDOLPH KOWNSLAR, b. ib. July 3, 1876;
1. Limestone County, Tex.; he is a farmer.

c. ELLEN JETT KOWNSLAR, b. Berryville,
Sep. 19, 1878; 1. Gindale, Texas.

d. ELIZABETH SINCLAIR KOWNSLAR, b. Berryville, Dec. 5, 1879; d. ib. Feb. 10, 1884.

e. CONRAD KOWNSLAR, b. ib. Aug. 11, 1886.

     f. HARRIOT HAMMOND KOWNSLAR, b. Roanoke, Jan. 7, 1892; d. Gindale, Texas, March 31, 1900.

(4). MARY LEWIS STRIBLING, b. Winchester, Aug. 25, 1856; d. ib. Sep. 23, 1856.

(5). WILLIAM McCORMICK STRIBLING, b. Staunton, Sep. 10, 1857; d. ib. Oct. 2, 1858.

(6). EDWARD McCORMICK STRIBLING, b. ib. June 1, 1859; d. Washington, D. C., March 25, 1892; m. Berryville, Jan. 11, 1883, *Lydia Kownslar* (b. ib. May 22, 1856; she is a sister of Randolph Kownslar mentioned above; l. ib.); he was a farmer near Berryville.

     a. RANDOLPH KOWNSLAR STRIBLING, b. Berryville, Oct. 23, 1883; d. ib. July 4, 1884.

     b. EDWARD McCORMICK STRIBLING, b. ib. June 4, 1885.

     c. JOHN WRIGHT STRIBLING, b. ib. April 5, 1887.

     d. ANNIE MAUDE STRIBLING, b. ib. April 5, 1887.

§33 II. TALIAFERRO STRIBLING, b. "Hopewell", about 1785; d. Clarke County, May 4, 1850, "aged 65"; m near Martinsburg, W. Va., Jan. 18, 1814, *Mary Tate*, his first cousin, (b. ib. in 1792; d. Washington, D. C., July 31, 1885, "aged 93"; see Note 2, §89); he was a physician, and lived first at Charlestown, W. Va , and then at Berryville.

1. MAGNUS TATE STRIBLING, b. Frederick County, Nov. 23, 1814; d. ib. Aug. 15, 1833.

2. ANN TALIAFERRO STRIBLING, b. ib. Dec. 21, 1817; d. Washington, D. C , June 8, 1854; m. "Roselawn", Frederick County, Nov. 7, 1837, *James Jones Miller* (b. Leesburg, Oct. 18, 1812; d. Denton, Ky., Dec. 5, 1898; p. Samuel Miller and Hannah Potter. He was connected with the Indian and Post Office Departments of the Government, and was later an editor and publisher at Lexington, Ky.).

§34   (1). MARY TALIAFERRO MILLER, b. "Roselawn", Dec. 6, 1840; m. Frankfort, Ky., Nov. 7, 1865,

DR. TALIAFERRO STRIBLING
33

Magnus Stribling Thompson, her first cousin; see §36.

(2). ANNIE WALLACE MILLER, b. Charlestown, W. Va., July 30, 1842; m. Ashland, Ky., Oct. 17, 1861, *Charles Scott Dodge Jones* (b. Sinsinewa Mound, Wis., Sep. 23, 1832; d. Dubuque, Iowa, Jan. 1889; p. Senator George Wallace Jones of Iowa, and Mary Josephine Gregoire; gr. p. Judge John Rice Jones of the Supreme Court of Missouri. He was a lawyer by profession; served on the staff of General Bushrod Johnson in the Confederate Army); 1. Washington, D. C.

    a. NANNIE STRIBLING JONES, b. and d. Richmond, in 1862.

    b. MARY JOSEPHINE JONES, b. near Richmond, in 1864; 1. Washington, D. C.

    c. KATHARINE STRIBLING JONES, b. Dubuque, Iowa, Feb. 8, 1867; m. Washington, D. C., Nov. 1, 1892, *Clarence Edward Dawson* (b. "Kendal Green", Md., July 31, 1869; p. Edward Matthews Dawson and Clara Cox; gr. p. Edward Matthews Dawson and Susan Hambleton Parrott—Dr. Christopher Christian Cox and Amanda Northrup. He has been Private Secretary to the Post Master General of the United States): 1. Chevy Chase, Md.

        (a). KATHARINE THELMA DAWSON, b. Washington, D. C., Nov. 22, 1895.

        (b). CLARENCE EDWARD DAWSON, b. ib. Jan. 18, 1899.

        (c). WALLACE STRIBLING DAWSON, b. Chevy Chase, Md., May 21, 1901.

    d. GEORGE WALLACE JONES, b. Sioux City, Iowa, in 1869; he is connected with the Post Office Department in Washington, D. C.

    e. MARY TALIAFERRO JONES, b. Dubuque, Iowa, Sep. 23, 1871; m. Washington, D. C., July 3, 1895, *John Josephus Lordan* (b. Galveston, Texas; he is a lawyer in New York City).

f. Eliza Ben Jones, b. Dubuque, Iowa, May 31, 1876; m. Baltimore, Md., Aug. 28, 1895, *Willis Owen Hohenstein* (b. in Missouri, Sep. 9, 1872; he is manager for Armour's establishment in Washington, D. C.).

    a. Willis Owen Hohenstein, b. ib. June 29, 1896.

    b. Ralph Wallace Hohenstein, b. ib. Jan. 16, 1900.

(3). Charles Taliaferro Miller, b. Charlestown, W. Va., Nov. 16, 1846; m. Cincinnati, O., June 9, 1879, *Fannie Colden Moore* of Cincinnati (p. Cadwallader Colden Moore and Mary Augusta Farrell; gr. p. John Moore and Lydia Stevens). He is a clerk in the Treasury Department at Washington, D. C.

    a. Charles Colden Miller, b. ib. April 7, 1882; e. Georgetown College; l. Washington, D. C.

(4). Ellwood Stribling Miller, b. Charlestown, W. Va., Oct. 8, 1848; m. Covington, Ky., Oct. 5, 1875, *Lollie Blanks Ward* (b. ib. June 27, 1856; p. Robert D. and Margaret Blanks Ward). He is a wholesale merchant at Covington, Ky.

    a. Robert Ward Miller, b. ib. Dec. 30, 1891.

    b. Virginia Stribling Miller, b. ib. Mch. 3, 1895.

§35   3. Catherine Mackey Stribling, b. Frederick Co., March 4, 1820; d. Sioux City, Iowa, May 14, 1874; m. "Roselawn", Frederick Co., Nov. 7, 1837, *William Broadus Thompson* (b. Culpeper Co., Aug. 8, 1816; d. Purcellville, July 28, 1883; p. Capt. Meriweather Thompson and Martha Broadus. He was a lawyer in Frederick County).

(1). William Taliaferro Thompson, b. "Roselawn", Oct. 26, 1840; e. University of Virginia; m. *1st.* Hancock, Md., Jan. 14, 1868, *Sarah Bridges* of that place (d. ib. April 27, 1869); m. *2nd.* Berryville, June 11, 1872, *Ann Eliza White*

(see MCILHANY FAMILY, §126); m. *3rd*. Mars
Bluff, S. C., July 28, 1885, *Mrs. Julia Adams-*
Gregg (b. Society Hill, S. C., Feb. 10, 1852; d.
Columbia, S. C., Nov. 25, 1898); m. *4th.* Charles-
ton, S. C., March 12, 1900, *Agnes Buist* (b.
Cheraw, S. C., June 11, 1875). He was Captain
of Co. D. 8th Missouri Cavalry, Army of Trans-
Mississippi, C. S. A. He is now pastor of the
Eckington Presbyterian Church in Washington,
D. C. The degree of D. D. was conferred upon
him by the University of Kansas in 1885. He
had one child by the first marriage, one by the
second, and two by the third.

> a. HENRY PERCIVAL PARR THOMPSON, b.
> Hancock, Md., Oct. 21, 1868; e. Hampden-
> Sidney College and Charleston Medical Col-
> lege; m. Washington, D. C., Nov. 14, 1894,
> *Helen Grace Lowdermilk* (b. Cumberland,
> Md., Jan. 14, 1871); he is a physician at
> Washington, D. C.
>
>> (a). WILLIAM PERCIVAL THOMPSON, b.
>> ib. Dec. 21, 1896.
>
> b. MARY ELLZEY THOMPSON, b. "Locust
> Thicket", Loudoun County, Aug. 28, 1873;
> 1. Washington, D. C.
>
> c. WILLIAM TALIAFERRO THOMPSON, b.
> Charleston, S. C., April 28, 1886; 1. Wash-
> ington, D. C.
>
> d. MAGNUS MCKEEVER THOMPSON, b.
> Charleston, S. C., March 6, 1892; d. ib. July
> 3, 1892.

(2). MARTHA LEE THOMPSON, b. "Roselawn", Dec.
31, 1844; m. *1st.* Berryville, May 18, 1867, *Philip*
Roach (b. Alexandria; d. in Texas in 1874); m.
2nd. Sioux City, Iowa, Nov. 7, 1876, *John Wesley*
Young (b. Boston, Mass., April 17, 1843; p.
John Wesley Young and Annie Damon. He is
a clerk at the Navy Yard in Washington).

> a. JOHN WESLEY YOUNG, b. Sioux City,
> Iowa, Aug. 30, 1877; he is connected with

a wholesale stationery firm in New York City.

b. MAGNUS TALIAFERRO YOUNG, b. Sioux City, Iowa, Nov. 2, 1878; he is in business in New York City.

c. GEORGE HARRY DAMON YOUNG, b. Sioux City, Iowa, April 21, 1882; l. Washington, D. C.

d. GEORGE WILLIE YOUNG, b. Sioux City, Iowa, Sep. 22, 1887; l. Washington, D. C.

§36   (3). MAGNUS STRIBLING THOMPSON, b. "Rose-lawn", July 31, 1846; m. Frankfort, Ky., Nov. 7, 1865, *Mary Taliaferro Miller*, his first cousin; see §34. He served through the entire Civil War, first as a courier to "Stonewall" Jackson, and then in the 35th Va. Cavalry. He is a clerk in the Navy Department at Washington.

§37   4. MARY ELIZABETH STRIBLING, b. "Roselawn", in 1827; d. "Clermont", near Berryville, July 14, 1853, "aged 26"; m. "Hopewell", Frederick County, Feb. 4, 1847, *Edward McCormick*, her second cousin; see MILTON FAMILY, §175.

§38 III. FRANCIS STRIBLING, b. "Hopewell", about 1787; d. "Montcalm", Loudoun Co., in 1828; m. *1st.* "Ithaca", Loudoun Co., Jan. 16, 1815, *Cecilia McIlhany* (see MCILHANY FAMILY, §132); m. *2nd.* "Kenilworth", Frederick Co., June 17, 1823, *Rebecca Littler* (d. about May 1, 1826; p. Samuel Littler and Ann Williams of Frederick County). He was at first a soldier, and afterwards a farmer at "Montcalm". About the time of his second marriage he was elected to the Virginia Legislature. The following record of his military service is found in the War Department at Washington: "Appointed Ensign, Rifle Regiment, 3 May, 1808; promoted second lieutenant 1 July, 1809; appointed first lieutenant, Light Artillery Regiment, 1 March, 1811; promoted Captain 1 November, 1813, and resigned May 1, 1816." He had five children by the first marriage and one by the second.

§39   1. MARGARET ANN STRIBLING, b. "Hopewell", Dec. 3, 1815; e. Woodstock and Leesburg; m. "Ithaca",

CAPT. FRANCIS STRIBLING
æ 38

Nov. 1, 1832, *Alexander Kilgour* (b. "Hollybush", St. Mary's Co., Md., Sep. 3, 1799; d. "The Pines", near Rockville, Md., Aug. 31, 1869; see §143); l. "The Pines".

   (1). WILLIAM KILGOUR, b. Rockville, Md., July 24, 1833; e. Charlotte Hall, and St. John's College, Annapolis, Md.; m. Rockville, Md., Oct. 24, 1858, *Rose Ellen Queen* (b. ib. June 9, 1834; d. ib. Sep. 9, 1886; p. Charles Joningham Queen and Maria Purcell). He was at one time State's Attorney in Alexandria; is now an editor and lawyer at Rockville, Md. He has served three terms at different times in the state Legislature.

     a. ANNIE STRIBLING KILGOUR, b. ib. Sep. 4, 1859; d. Alexandria, June 20, 1877.

     b. MARY CARTER KILGOUR, b. Rockville, Md. Jan. 2, 1863; l. ib.

   (2). CECILIA STRIBLING KILGOUR, b. ib. Jan. 8, 1835; d. "Clifton", Jan. 16, 1902; e. Brookeville Female Academy; m. "The Pines", Oct. 27, 1863, *Samuel Jones* (b. near Rockville, Md., July 31, 1820; d. "Clifton", near Rockville, Md., Sep. 14, 1891; p. John and Katherine Jones).

     a. FRANCIS KILGOUR JONES, b. ib. Nov. 7, 1864; d. ib. Jan. 10, 1898.

     b. SAMUEL MADDOX JONES, b. ib. Jan. 31, 1865; studied law at Columbian University, Washington, D. C., and is practicing in Baltimore, Md.

     c. MARGARET ALEXANDER JONES, b. "Clifton", Dec. 23, 1867; e. Academy of the Visitation, Frederick City, Md.; l. "Clifton".

     d. WILLIAM KILGOUR JONES, b. ib. Feb. 20, 1871; l. ib.

     e. CATHERINE JHON JONES, b. ib. June 18, 1873; e. Academy of the Visitation, Frederick City, Md.; m. Rockville, Md., March 8, 1899, *Albert J. Allder;* he is farming at Woodbridge, Prince William County; they have two children.

        f. JAMES DECATUR JONES, b. "Clifton", June 22, 1878; d. ib. June 2, 1880.

§40   (3). FRANCIS STRIBLING KILGOUR, b. Rockville, Md., Oct. 10, 1836; e. ib.; m. Loudoun County, Nov. 22, 1870, *Margaret McIlhany Heaton*, his first cousin (see § 44). He served through the entire civil war in General Rosser's Brigade, 35th Va. Cavalry. He is farming at "The Pines", Montgomery County, Md.

        a. MATTIE CHILTON KILGOUR, b. ib. Sep. 7, 1871; d. ib. Jan. 31, 1896.

        b. CECILIA DECATUR KILGOUR, b. ib. Nov. 7, 1873; e. Wesleyan Female Institute, Staunton; l. "The Pines."

        c. JANE HAGUE KILGOUR, b. ib. Mch. 31, 1876; e. Rockville Seminary; l. "The Pines."

        d. ALEXANDER KILGOUR, b. ib. Nov. 9, 1878; d. ib. Oct. 27, 1900.

        e. LYDIA HEATON KILGOUR, b. ib. April 26, 1880; m. Potomac Church, Montgomery Co., Md., Aug. 7, 1901, *Dr. Ralph Francis Stribling Porter*, her second cousin (see § 42).

        f. ELLA NEWTON KILGOUR, b "The Pines", Feb. 28, 1885; l. ib.

    (4). MARY LOUISA KILGOUR, b. Rockville, Md., July 21, 1838; d. ib. August 11, 1839.

    (5). CHARLES JOURDAN KILGOUR, b. ib. March 30, 1840; d. Washington, D. C., Oct. 1, 1863.

    (6). MARTHA MATILDA KILGOUR, b. "The Pines", May 14, 1842; d. Rockville, Md., Dec. 24, 1900; e. Rockville Seminary; m. "The Pines", Feb. 21, 1865, *Capt. Alexander Wheeler Chilton* (b. Kingston, Canada, Feb. 19, 1837; d. Alexandria, Jan. 8, 1882; p. Alexander Chilton of Canada. He was a Captain in the U. S. Army, and at the time of his death was city Judge of Alexandria).

    (7). SARAH EDGERTON KILGOUR, b. "The Pines", Feb. 5, 1845; e. Rockville Seminary, and Maryland State Normal School in Baltimore; l. "The Pines".

(8). VIRGINIA KILGOUR, b. ib. Dec. 19, 1847; e.
Washington, D. C.; d. Baltimore, Md., Oct. 27,
1878; m. "The Pines", Oct. 27, 1875, *Charles
Oscar Vandeventer* (b. "Locust Grove", Loudoun Co., Oct. 10, 1849; p. Washington Vandeventer and Cecilia Braden of Loudoun Co.; gr.
p. Joseph Vandeventer. He was a civil engineer
with the Western Maryland R. R., and is now
living at Hagerstown, Md.).

> a. BRADEN VANDEVENTER, b. "Locust
> Grove", May 5, 1878; e. Danville Military
> Institute and Washington and Lee Universi-
> ty; is practicing law at Newport News.

(9). ALEXANDER KILGOUR, b. "The Pines", April
8, 1855; e. Washington, D. C. He was for some
years State's Attorney of Montgomery County,
Md.; is now practicing law at Rockville, Md.

§41   2. FRANCIS JAMES STRIBLING, b. "Hopewell", Feb.
3, 1817; e. Winchester; d. Parkersburg, W. Va., Nov.
19, 1889; m. "Wood Grove", Loudoun Co., in Nov.
1838, *Amanda Mary Ann Heaton* (b. ib. June 8, 1821;
d. Parkersburg, W. Va., June 22, 1875; p. Dr. Jonathan Heaton and Patience Osborne; gr. p. Dr. James
Heaton and Hannah Smith). In Loudoun County
he was Captain of a militia company. He was a
member of the city council in Parkersburg, W. Va.,
and was for more than fifty years connected with the
B. & O. Railroad at different places.

(1). MARGARET ELIZABETH STRIBLING, b. "Wood
Grove", Oct. 5, 1839; graduated at the Wheeling
Female College; m. Parkersburg, W. Va., Feb.
29, 1876, *James Lafayette Hugh Longest* (b.
Westmoreland Co., Oct. 28, 1824; p. Louis
L'Ongest and Mary Pitts. He is farming at
"Nauvoo", near Bon Air).

> a. AMA STRIBLING LONGEST, b. ib. March
> 26, 1877; graduated at the Richmond Female
> Seminary; m. Washington, D. C., Dec. 12,
> 1899, *Lynnwood Cheilds Moody* (b. Manches-
> ter, Jan. 12, 1875); l. "Nauvoo".

(2). CECILIA MCILHANY STRIBLING, b. Loudoun
Co.; e. Fetterman, W. Va.; 1. Pittsburg, Penn.

(3). JONATHAN HEATON STRIBLING, b. "Wood
Grove", March 7, 1846; e. Parkersburg, W. Va.,
and Cincinnati, O.; d. Parkersburg, W. Va.,
Mch. 17, 1885; m. ib. May 19, 1880, *Bettie Neal*
(b. ib. Aug. 15, 1858; p. Geo. W. Neal and Carrie
McKinley; gr. p. Capt. Jas. Neal. She has since
married Mr. George Franklin Bowles of New
Orleans, La.). He was a merchant in Parkersburg, W. Va.

    a. CARRIE HEATON STRIBLING, b. ib. Nov.
    26, 1882; is a student at the Sophie New-
    comb College, New Orleans, La.

(4). MARY JEANNETTE STRIBLING, b. Cumberland, Md.; e. Parkersburg and Point Pleasant,
W. Va.; 1. Pittsburg, Penn.

(5). ERASMUS MORTIMER STRIBLING, b. Fetterman, W. Va.; e. Parkersburg, W. Va.; m. ib.
Lottie Ingold of that place. He is connected
with the B. & O. Railroad at Philadelphia, Penn.

    a. PERCY STRIBLING, b. Parkersburg, W.
    Va., June 26, 1883; 1. ib.

    b. FLORENCE STRIBLING, b. ib. March 19,
    1886; 1. Pittsburg, Penn.

    c. EDNA MAY STRIBLING, b. Parkersburg,
    W. Va., in May, 1888; d. ib. in 1890.

§42   3. ERASMUS MORTIMER STRIBLING, b. "Ithaca", Loudoun County, June 13, 1818; e. in Kentucky; d. Lou-
dounville, O., Apr. 15, 1857; m. Springfield, O., Oct.
11, 1848, *Mrs. Caroline Mary Mott–Wilson* (b. Mt.
Vernon, O., Nov. 19, 1821; p. Samuel Mott and Lu-
rena Newell of Connecticut; gr. p. John Mott, of the
Revolutionary War, and Mary Rowley of Connecticut
—Riverius Newell, also of the Revolution, and Sarah
Peek of Connecticut; 1. Chicago, Ill.). He was chief
civil engineer for the S. M. V. and P. R. R., with his
home at Springfield, Ohio.

    (1). ALBERT STRIBLING, b. ib. July 28, 1849; d.
    ib. Aug. 23, 1850.

(2). MARY FRY VIRGINIA STRIBLING, b. ib. Dec. 29, 1851; e. ib. and at the Mendota Lutheran College. She has been instructor in music at Cornell College, Mt. Vernon, Iowa.

(3). CAROLINE CECILIA STRIBLING, b. Springfield, O., Sep. 8, 1855; e. ib. and at the Mendota Lutheran College; m. Mendota, Ill., Oct. 21, 1873, *John Alexander Porter* (b. La Salle Co., Ill., Oct. 21, 1852; p. Peter Latchair Porter and Mary Smith; gr. p. John Porter and Ann Latchair—James Smith and Sarah Eaken); 1. Chicago, Ill.

    a. RALPH FRANCIS STRIBLING PORTER, b. Fairfield, Ia., Nov 22, 1875; e. Chicago and Eureka, Kan., and took the degree of M. D. at Rush Medical College, Chicago, in 1897; m. Potomac Church, Montgomery Co., Md., Aug. 7, 1901, *Lydia Heaton Kilgour*, his second cousin (see § 40). He was Asst. Surgeon of the 2nd Illinois Infantry during the Spanish war, and is now stationed in the Philippines as a surgeon in the U. S. Army.

4. ELIZABETH STRIBLING, b. "Ithaca" about May 1, 1820; d. ib. in infancy.

§43   5. CECILIA McILHANY STRIBLING, b. ib. Apr. 5, 1822; e. in Fairfax County; d. "Sunnyside", Loudoun Co., Aug. 8, 1862; m. "The Pines", Montgomery Co., Md., Jan. 21, 1842, *Dr. James Decatur Heaton* (b. "Exedra", Loudoun Co., April 25, 1816; d ib. Feb. 21, 1859; p. Dr. James Heaton and Lydia Osborne, a sister of Patience Osborne, § 41; gr. p. John Heaton—Abner and Patience Osborne).

    (1). ALBERT HEATON, b. "Exedra", Aug. 31, 1844; d. Washington, Va., Apr. 18, 1864, of sickness contracted during service in the 8th Va. Infantry, C. S. A.

    (2). TOWNSEND HEATON, b. "Exedra", Sept. 1, 1846; took the M. D. degree at the Univ. of Pa.; d. Hamilton, Dec. 16, 1883; m. Baltimore, Md., Oct. 30, 1873, *Florence Janney* (b. Hardy Co, W. Va., Aug. 30, 1848; p. Geo. W. Janney and

Mary Compher of Loudoun Co.; gr. p. John Janney and Susan Wells of Loudoun Co. She has since married a Mr. Mercer and lives near Hamilton). He was a courier to Gen. D. H. Hill in the early part of the Civil War, and was afterwards a member of Mosby's Command, 43rd Va. Cavalry. He practiced medicine in Michigan.

> a.   FLORENCE JANNEY HEATON, b. Ishpeming, Mich., April 27, 1878; e. Baltimore Woman's College; l. near Hamilton.

§44
(3).   MARGARET MCILHANY HEATON, b. "Exedra", Aug. 23, 1848; e. Leesburg; m. Loudoun County, Nov. 22, 1870, *Francis Stribling Kilgour*, her first cousin; see § 40.

(4).   FRANCIS ERASMUS STRIBLING HEATON, b. "Exedra", Sept. 8, 1850; d. Leesburg, Feb. 8, 1868.

(5).   LYDIA HEATON, b. "Exedra", June 5, 1853; e. Winchester; d. Pæonian Springs, Sept. 9, 1885.

(6).   CECILIA DECATUR HEATON, b. "Exedra", Nov. 29, 1857; e. Hamilton; m. ib. Dec. 23, 1880, *Rodney Walter Braden* (b. "Elmwood", Loudoun County, Sept. 12, 1858; p. Rodney C. Braden and Eliza Ann Vandeventer; gr. p. John Braden and Mary Stephens—Joseph Vandeventer and Mary Means. He is farming at "Elmwood".).

> a.   TOWNSEND HEATON BRADEN, b. ib. April 26, 1884; d. ib. Nov. 12, 1885.
>
> b.   OSCAR STEPHEN BRADEN, b. ib. April 21, 1886.
>
> c.   ALBERT VANDEVENTER BRADEN, b. ib. February 19, 1888.
>
> d.   WALTER DOUGLAS BRADEN, b. ib. Sept. 11, 1891.

6.   ANNE ELIZABETH STRIBLING, b. Frederick County, March 30, 1824; l. Mt. Jackson.

IV.   MAGNUS TATE STRIBLING, b. "Hopewell", about 1789; he served in the war of 1812 in a troop of horse, then sailed for several years, and afterwards engaged in the

flour business in Alexandria. He died unmarried about
1835.

§45 V. SIGISMUND STRIBLING, b. "Hopewell", about 1791; d.
Frederick Co., now Clarke Co., in 1822; m. ib. Nov. 7,
1820, *Sarah Elizabeth Taliaferro Ware* (b. ib. about 1797;
d. ib. April 16, 1878; see Note 3, § 91). He was a lawyer
and lived in Frederick County. His only child was—
1. SIGISMUNDA STRIBLING, b. ib. in Aug. 1821; d.
Orkney Springs, Sept. 16, 1879; m. Clarke County,
June 13, 1848, *Charles Edmund Kimball* (b. Baltimore,
Md., Dec. 22, 1823; d. Macon, Ga., May 4, 1887; p.
Leonard Kimball and Sarah Yates Smith; gr. p. Edmund and Rebecca Kimball of Bradford, Mass.,—
Charles and Mary Yates Smith of Lancaster, Pa. He
was a Major in the Confederate Army, and a farmer in
Clarke county).
(1). THEODORE HORATIO KIMBALL, b. Hardwicke, Clarke County, Nov. 8, 1854; d. Penseco-
la, Fla., Dec. 29, 1900; m. Independence, Kan.,
Feb. 16, 1886, *Mary Nolte* of that place.
Their only child,
a. WILLIE KIMBALL, died in infancy.
(2). WILLIAM WARE KIMBALL, b. Hardwicke,
August 3, 1857; e. Va. Theological Seminary; m.
Macon, Ga., June 5, 1889, *Violet Wrigley* (b.
ib. July 11, 1869). He is a minister of the Episcopal Church at Darlington, Md.
a. ANNIE LUCY KIMBALL, b. Milledgeville,
Ga., July 9, 1890.
b. FLORETTA KIMBALL, b. Versailes, Ky.,
July 31, 1892.
c. WILLIAM WARE KIMBALL, b. Waycross,
Ga., Oct. 9, 1894; d. ib. Oct. 15, 1894.

§46 VI. MARY TATE STRIBLING, b. "Hopewell", about 1793;
d. "Woodland", June 2, 1820; m. "Hopewell", Jan. 14,
1813, *Col. James Crawford* (b. Augusta Co., in 1787; d.
"Woodland", May 11, 1855, "aged 68"; p. George Crawford; he was a lawyer and for a long time Presiding Justice
of the County, and lived at "Woodland", near Staunton;
he served in the war of 1812; he married secondly Mrs.

Margaret Allen Bell–Crawford, by whom he had ten children).

1. FRANCIS GEORGE CRAWFORD, b. "Woodland", Dec. 23, 1813; d. Greenwood, Miss., about 1856, unmarried.

§47   2. ERASMUS STRIBLING CRAWFORD, b. "Woodland," March 16, 1815; d. Memphis, Tenn., Feb. 7,1865; m. Christian County, Ky., Sept. 4, 1840, *Elvira Ann West* (b. ib. Nov. 12, 1816; d. Memphis, Tenn., August 1, 1896); he was a wholesale grocer at Vicksburg, Miss., till 1859, when he removed to Memphis, Tenn.

(1). MARY STRIBLING CRAWFORD, b. Vicksburg, Miss., Nov. 15, 1842; d. St. Louis, Mo., March 11, 1891; m. Memphis, Tenn., June 29, 1868, *Captain Charles Tilghman Biser* (b. Burkitsville, Md., about 1837; d. St. Louis, Mo., March 13, 1896; he was a Captain in the Confederate Army, and afterwards engaged in the real estate business).

a. WEST CRAWFORD BISER, b. Memphis, Tenn., May 20, 1870; he is a lawyer in St. Louis, Mo.

(2). WEST JAMES CRAWFORD, b. Madison County, Miss., Nov. 1, 1844; m. Memphis, Tenn., Nov. 11, 1874, *Anna Louise Thompson* (b. Chickasaw County, Miss., May 20, 1850). He is President of the Commercial Appeal Publishing Company, Memphis, Tenn.

a. ERASMUS STRIBLING CRAWFORD, b. ib. August 13, 1875.

b. KATE THOMPSON CRAWFORD, b. ib. Dec. 4, 1877.

c. MARIANNE WEST CRAWFORD, b ib. June, 21, 1886.

(3). ERASMUS STRIBLING CRAWFORD, b. Vicksburg, Miss., in 1846; d. ib. in infancy.

(4). BETTIE ANN CRAWFORD, b. ib. May 15, 1849; m. Memphis, Tenn., Sep. 3, 1872, *Richard Dudley Jordan* (b. Hampton, Oct. 7, 1842; he is a lawyer); 1. Memphis, Tenn.

      a. LOUISE CRAWFORD JORDAN, b. ib. June 7, 1873; m. ib. April 9, 1902, *William Louis Davis* (b. August 13, 1871; he is a wholesale dry goods merchant in Nashville, Tenn.).

      b. LAURA BANKS JORDAN, b. Memphis,Tenn., Feb. 3, 1875.

      c. ELVIRA JORDAN, b. ib. Jan. 22, 1879.

      d. RICHARD DUDLEY JORDAN, b. ib. April 27, 1887.

      e. WEST CRAWFORD JORDAN, b. ib. April 24, 1889.

  (5). VIRGINIA CRAWFORD, b. Vicksburg, Miss., in 1851; d. ib. in infancy.

  (6). IDA FLORENCE CRAWFORD, b. ib. May 1, 1853; d. Memphis, Tenn., Sept. 5, 1868.

  (7). ELVIRA LOUISE CRAWFORD, b. Vicksburg, Miss., March 23, 1856; m. Memphis, Tenn., Jan. 13, 1881, *Julius Alexander Taylor* (b. La Grange, Tenn., Feb. 6, 1840; d. Memphis, Tenn., August 1, 1895; he was a lawyer); 1. ib.

      a. MARGARET TAYLOR, b. ib. March 14, 1882.

      b. WARREN CRAWFORD TAYLOR, b. ib. Sept. 23, 1885.

      c. LOUISE FOWLER TAYLOR, b. ib. August 15, 1889.

§48   3. MAGNUS WILLIAM CRAWFORD, b. "Woodland", April 18, 1817; d. Louisville, Ky., Nov. 12, 1896; m. *1st.* Seville, Madison Co., January 16, 1837, *Margaret Mildred Simms* (b. ib. March 5, 1818; d. Locust Grove, Greene County, Sept. 14, 1863; p. William and Eliza Simms); m. *2nd.* Stanardsville, Greene County, Jan. 10, 1867, *Mrs. Emily Amanda White* (b. Seville, Feb. 10, 1824; d. Locust Grove, in Aug. 1879; she was a sister of his first wife); he was a farmer, and lived in Madison and Greene counties; he had seven children by his first marriage, none by the second.

  (1). JAMES WILLIAM CRAWFORD, b. Augusta County, Dec. 28, 1838; m. Culpeper County, November 27, 1877, *Lucy Barbour Gaines* (b.

Locust Hill, Culpeper County, February 15, 1855); 1. Cincinnati, O ; he is a salesman.

- a. GEORGE LEE CRAWFORD, b. Culpeper, August 19, 1878.
- b. FRANCES KENNETH CRAWFORD, b. Hurricane, W. Va., November 30, 1883.
- c. FLORA VIRGINIA CRAWFORD, b. Richmond, Ky., Nov. 7, 1887.
- d. JAMES EDWIN CRAWFORD, b. Cincinnati, O., Sept. 1, 1892.

(2). MARY ELIZA CRAWFORD, b. Augusta County, Dec. 3, 1841; m. Charlottesville, March 15, 1882, *Joseph William May* (b. Amherst County, June 6, 1846; his first wife was her sister Margaret Flora; see below); 1. Indianapolis, Ind.

(3). FRANK HENRY CRAWFORD, b. near Staunton, April 3, 1843; d. Locust Grove, August 17, 1863.

(4). MARGARET FLORA CRAWFORD, b. near Staunton, June 11, 1845; d. Albemarle County, June 12, 1881; m. Greene County, May 7, 1878, *Joseph William May*, who afterwards married her sister Mary; see above.

- a. WILLIAM ALFRED MAY, b. Orange County, June 10, 1879; d. ib. June 11, 1879.
- b. CORA LEE MAY, b. Albemarle County, Dec. 25, 1880; d. Catlettsburg, Ky., Nov. 20, 1881.

(5). MAGNUS SIMMS CRAWFORD, b. near Staunton, in 1848; d. Richmond, Nov. 20, 1895; m. Greene County, Dec. 22, 1866, *Eliza Virenda Simms*, his first cousin (b. ib. March 21, 1844; d. ib. June 28, 1870); they had no children; he served with Col. Mosby in the Confederate Army.

(6). ERASMUS STRIBLING CRAWFORD, b. near Staunton, Feb. 1, 1852; m. Fairfield, Kanawha County, W. Va., Sep. 23, 1883, *Nancy Jane Porter* (b. ib. June 20, 1866); he is farming at Fairfield, W. Va.

a. ANNIE MILDRED CRAWFORD, b. ib. Aug.
5, 1884.

b. WILLIAM HENRY CRAWFORD, b. ib. July
28, 1886.

c. FRANK LEE CRAWFORD, b. ib. May 6,
1890; d. ib. August 22, 1890.

d. KENNA CRAWFORD, b. ib. July 15, 1891.

e. MARY MAY CRAWFORD, b. ib. March 22,
1894.

(7). AMANDA MILDRED CRAWFORD, b. near Staunton, Feb. 24, 1855; d. ib. April 7, 1855.

4. JAMES SAMUEL CRAWFORD, b. "Woodland", Aug.
29, 1818; d. in Texas, in Dec. 1853, leaving a widow
and one daughter, of whom nothing is known.

§49   5. MARY TATE CRAWFORD, b. "Woodland", Jan. 19,
1820; d. Washington, Rappahannock County, Va.,
April 16, 1860; m. near Staunton, Sept. 3, 1840,
Jechonias Yancy Menefee (b. near Sperryville. April 15,
1815; d. Washington, Va., Nov. 9, 1888. He was a
lawyer at Washington, being for some time Commonwealth's Attorney for the County).

(1). MARY ELLA MENEFEE, b. Washington, Va.,
May 4, 1842; m. ib. Sept. 26, 1857, *William
Franklin Anderson* (b. Rappahannock County,
June 2, 1840. He served through the Civil War
in the Confederate Army. He was formerly a
merchant, and is now paymaster of the West Va.
Pulp and Paper Company, at Covington, Va.).

a. MARY STRIBLING ANDERSON, b. Washing-
ton, Va., July 27, 1868; m. ib. Nov. 24, 1897,
Rev. Joseph Howard Gibbons (b. Washington
D. C., Dec. 22, 1870; he is Rector of the
Episcopal Church at Point Pleasant, W. Va.).

(a). MARY ELLA GIBBONS, b. Stafford
County, Dec. 19, 1898.

(b). JOSEPH HOWARD GIBBONS, b. Covington, Feb. 20, 1901.

b. SARAH JOSEPHINE ANDERSON, b. Washington, Va., April 30, 1870.

   c. BESSIE CARROLL ANDERSON, b. Washington, Va., Nov. 2, 1871; m. Winston, N. C., Dec. 18, 1895, *David Lincoln Luke* (b. Wilmington, Del., May 14, 1865); 1. Piedmont, W. Va.

     (a). JEAN ANDERSON LUKE, b. ib. Dec. 4, 1896.

     (b). DOROTHY LUKE, b. ib. Dec. 11, 1897.

     (c). DAVID LINCOLN LUKE, b. ib. Jan. 5, 1899.

     (d). MARY ANDERSON LUKE, b. ib. June 28, 1901.

   d. DORA MENEFEE ANDERSON, b. Washington, Va., March 27, 1875.

   e. WILLIAM FRANKLIN ANDERSON, b. Hawthorne, March 28, 1881.

   f. IDA MOFFETT ANDERSON, b. ib. Dec. 2, 1882.

(2). HENRY ST. CYR MENEFEE, b. Washington, Va., June 18, 1844. He served in the 6th Va. Cavalry and with Mosby's Men in the Civil War. He is now a lawyer at Washington, Va.

(3). JAMES CRAWFORD MENEFEE, b. ib. in 1846. He is farming at "Avondale", near Washington, Va.

(4). VIRGINIA FLORENCE MENEFEE, b. Washington, Va., July 8, 1848; 1. ib.

(5). FRANCIS GEORGE MENEFEE, b. ib. Dec. 25, 1850; graduated at the V. M. I.; m. *Mrs. Sarah Skinner* of Santa Cruz, Cal., where he is cashier of the Santa Cruz County Bank.

(6). ELVIRA MENEFEE, b. ib. in 1853; d. ib. in 1854.

(7). IDA STRIBLING MENEFEE, b. ib. March 12, 1854; m. ib. Oct. 1, 1878, *Horatio Gates Moffett* (b. "Glenwood", near ib., March 30, 1854; he is a lawyer; was at one time Commonwealth's Attorney for the County); 1. "Glenwood".

    a. WILLIAM FRANKLIN MOFFETT, b. Haw-
thorne, Sep. 28, 1879.

    b. MARY LOU MOFFETT, b. "Glenwood",
Sept. 3, 1880.

    c. HENRY ST. CYR MOFFETT, b. Washing-
ton, Va., Nov. 5, 1883.

    d. NETTIE GATES MOFFETT, b. "Glenwood",
July 15, 1892; d. ib. August 20, 1892.

    e. HORATIO GATES MOFFETT, b. ib. March
21, 1894.

  (8). DORA MENEFEE, b. Washington, Va., Aug.
19, 1858; 1. ib.

  (9). NITA MCDONALD MENEFEE, b. ib. Nov. 10,
1860; d. ib. Dec. 16, 1898.

§50 VII. NANCY TATE STRIBLING, b. "Hopewell", June 30,
1795; d. "Norwood", Clarke County, Dec. 24, 1847; m.
"Hopewell", Sept. 20, 1815, *Lewis Neill* (b. Frederick
County, May 9, 1794; d. "Norwood", July 28, 1836; p.
Joseph Neill and Rebecca McPherson; he was a merchant,
and a farmer at "Norwood").

  1. JOSEPH LEWIS NEILL, b. ib. Dec. 9, 1817; d. ib.
Oct. 1, 1818.

  2. WILLIAM HENRY NEILL, b. ib. Oct. 1, 1819; d.
ib. July 24, 1820.

  3. A daughter, b. and d. ib. August 15, 1821.

  4. LEWIS NEILL, b. ib. May 13, 1823; e. West Point
Military Academy; was a Lieutenant in the U. S.
Army; d. in Mexico, Jan. 13, 1850, of a wound re-
ceived in the Mexican War.

§51   5. SIGISMUND STRIBLING NEILL, b. "Norwood",
Oct. 18, 1825; d. Berryville, Nov. 23, 1895; e. University of Va., and Medical Department of the University of Penn.; m. Winchester, June 11, 1850, *Catherine Snickers Baldwin* (b. Winchester, March 31,
1827; d. Berryville, Dec. 23, 1890; see Note 3, §93);
he was a surgeon in the Confederate Army, and afterwards a physician at Berryville.

§52   (1). CATHERINE STUART NEILL, b. "Norwood",
April 27, 1851; m. Berryville, Oct. 19, 1898,
William Hierome Thomas Lewis (b. "The Rocks",

Jefferson County, W. Va., April 30, 1832; see §88); 1. Myerstown, Jefferson County, W. Va.

(2). ANNIE REBECCA NEILL, b. "Norwood", August 20, 1853; d. Berryville, July 14, 1894.

(3). LEWIS NEILL, b. ib. Jan. 16, 1858; d ib. March 26, 1863.

(4). MARY BALDWIN NEILL, b. ib. April 5, 1860; d. ib. May 23, 1885.

(5). JOHN MACKEY BALDWIN NEILL, b. ib. April 28, 1866; e. Roanoke College; m. Berryville, Dec. 19, 1895, *Ellen Douglas MacDonald* (b. Bullitt County, Ky., Oct. 3, 1870); he is deputy clerk of the county and circuit courts at Berryville

    a. JOHN BALDWIN NEILL, b ib. Oct 3. 1896.

    b. WILLIAM MACDONALD NEILL, b. ib. Sept. 28, 1901.

§53   6. ANN REBECCA NEILL, b. "Norwood", January 13, 1830; d. Clarke County, July 31, 1853; m. ib. in 1852, *Thomas McCormick* of "Elmington", as his second wife; see §200.

    7. MARY NEILL, b. "Norwood", Oct 2, 1831; d. Frederick County, Nov. 26, 1895; m. Clarke County, Feb. 17, 1857, *Joseph Marx Barton* (b. Richmond, March 26, 1835; p. Richard W. Barton and Caroline Marx of Frederick County; gr. p. Richard Peters Barton and Martha Walker; 1. near Kernstown).

(1). ANN NEILL BARTON, b. Frederick County, Nov. 22, 1857; d. ib. Jan. 8, 1879.

§54   (2). SAMUEL MARX BARTON, b. ib. May 9, 1859; graduated as A. B. and Ph. D. at the University of Va.; m. Winchester, Dec. 28, 1897, *Mary Millicent Tidball* (b. ib. March 18, 1866); he is Professor of Mathematics in the University of the South, Sewanee, Tenn.

    a. MARY NEILL BARTON, b. Winchester, March 20, 1899.

    b. HELEN THRUSTON BARTON, b. Sewanee, Tenn., July 2, 1900.

(3). LEWIS NEILL BARTON, b. Frederick County,
Dec. 15, 1860; m. Winchester, April 20, 1892,
Elizabeth Cover (b. Baltimore County, Md., Oct.
24, 1868; d. Winchester, Dec. 11, 1897); he is a
banker in Winchester.

   a. THOMAS COVER BARTON, b. ib. April 5,
      1893.

   b. LEWIS NEILL BARTON, b. ib. Nov. 11,
      1894.

   c. JOSEPH MARX BARTON, b. ib. March 14,
      1896.

(4). CAROLINE MARX BARTON, b. Frederick
County, Oct. 18, 1862; l. near Kernstown.

(5). WILLIAM BARTON, b. ib. May 17, 1864; d.
ib. Feb. 3, 1865.

(6). JOSEPH MARX BARTON, b. ib. Jan. 19, 1866;
d. ib. Nov. 11, 1881.

(7). CHARLES MARX BARTON, b. ib. June 14,
1867; d. ib. Jan. 28, 1868.

(8). FREDERICK MARX BARTON, b. ib. Nov. 28,
1868; m. Carlisle, Penn., Oct. 20, 1897, *Rose
Beula Getter* (b. "Maple Grove", Cumberland
County, Penn., Feb. 25, 1874); he is agent for the
Cumberland Valley R. R. at Carlisle, Penn.

§55 VIII. THOMAS STRIBLING, b. "Hopewell", about 1797; d.
New Orleans, La., in Nov. 1833; m. near Winchester,
June 17, 1823, *Rachel Ann Littler* (b. ib. in 1806; d. Spring-
field, Ill., June 5, 1868.) He was a merchant, but at
the time of his death was farming. He was murdered in
New Orleans while on his way to Texas to buy land.

   1. MARIA LOUISA STRIBLING, b. near Winchester, in
      Feb. 1826; d. Winchester, Jan. 1, 1848.

   2. PORTIA HOPKINS STRIBLING, b. Winchester, Sept.
      9, 1828; l. Springfield, Ill.; m. Lexington, Ky., Oct.
      29, 1850, *Andrew Jackson Barry* (b. ib. June 6, 1825;
      d. Columbus, Ky., in the summer of 1865, where he
      was practicing law; his father, William T. Barry, was
      Postmaster General under President Andrew Jackson).

      (1). WILLIAM TAYLOR BARRY, b. Woodford
         County, Ky., Sept. 3, 1851; d. ib. Nov. 25, 1854.

(2). SIGISMUND STRIBLING BARRY, b. Lexington, Ky., Dec. 28, 1852; d. Normal, Ill., Sept. 23, 1872.

(3). ARMISTEAD MASON BARRY, b. Woodford County, Ky., June 16, 1854; m. Springfield, Ill., June 20, 1888, *Emily Gertrude Canfield* (b. Port Elizabeth, N. J., Oct. 8, 1850); he is a retired farmer, living at Columbus, Ky.

    a. EMILY GERTRUDE BARRY, b. Minneapolis, Minn., April 15, 1889.

    b. ARMISTEAD MASON BARRY, b. ib. Oct. 7, 1890.

    c. MARY VREDENBURGH BARRY, b. ib. Sept. 6, 1892.

(4). LOUISA STRIBLING BARRY, b. Newport, Ky., March 31, 1856; d. Springfield, Ill., July 9, 1902; m. ib. April 30, 1884, *Augustus Louis Ulrich* (b. ib. August 2, 1854; he is a grain dealer at Springfield, Ill.).

    a. BARRY STRIBLING ULRICH, b. Chicago, Ill., July 6, 1888.

    b. PORTIA MARGARET ULRICH, b. ib. Sept. 9, 1889.

    c. EDWRAD VON REISENCAMP ULRICH, b. ib. Sept. 29, 1893.

(5). WILLIAM TAYLOR BARRY, b. Columbus, Ky., Nov. 26, 1858; m. *1st*. Chicago, Ill., March 30, 1891, *Lillian Morse* (b. Mobile, Ala., Jan. 5, 1866; d. Florence, Ariz., Feb. 4, 1894); m. *2nd*. San Francisco, Cal., May 28, 1901, *Julia Victoria Morse*, a sister of his first wife (b. Mobile, Ala., Sept. 16, 1873); he is a physician at Salinas, California.

    a. WILLIAM TAYLOR BARRY, b. San Bernadino, Cal., Jan. 15, 1892.

    b. DAVID MORSE BARRY, b. Florence, Arizona, Jan. 12, 1894.

(6). CATHARINE MASON BARRY, b. Columbus, Ky., Dec. 22, 1861; m. Chicago, Ill., Oct. 17, 1893, *Alfred Charles Le Baron*; l. Springfield, Ill.

      a. MASON ETHELBERT LE BARON, b. San
      Bernardino, Cal., April 28, 1895.

      b. LOUIS ULRICH LE BARON, b. San Jose,
      Cal., Dec. 27, 1897.

3. SIGISMUND TAYLOR STRIBLING, b. near Huntington, W. Va., Nov. 22, 1830; d. Point Lookout, Aug.
22, 1864.

4. MARGARET ANN STRIBLING, b. near Huntington,
W. Va., July 20, 1834; d. Richmond, Va., Jan. 21,
1884; m. *1st.* Lexington, Ky., Oct. 29, 1850, *Samuel
Preston Humphreys* (b. in Kentucky, June 28, 1828;
d. in New Mexico, about 1856); m. *2nd.* Springfield,
Ill., August 28, 1876, *Henry Emery Coleman Basker-
ville* (b. Lombardy Grove, Va., Oct. 14, 1817; d. Richmond, Jan. 14, 1900; he was a merchant in early life,
but retired from active business about the time of his
marriage).

    (1). DAVID CARLYSLE HUMPHREYS, b. Woodford
    County, Ky., January 13, 1852; d. Santa Barbara,
    Cal., July 6, 1893.

    (2). THOMAS STRIBLING HUMPHREYS, b. Wood-
    ford County, Ky., Oct. 31, 1853; d. Jacksonville,
    Fla., Nov. 28, 1893.

§56 IX. MARGARET PERRY STRIBLING, b. "Hopewell", April
11, 1800; d. Mt. Jackson, July 18, 1861; m. "Hopewell",
May 28, 1823, *Joel Pennybacker* (b. Shenandoah County,
August 9, 1793; d. Mt. Jackson, April 5, 1862; he was a
lawyer and served several terms as State Senator. His
house, called "The White House", was situated at Pine
Forge, four miles south of Mt. Jackson).

1. MARY CRAWFORD STRIBLING PENNYBACKER, b.
Woodstock, March 22, 1824; d. Lebanon, Pa., Oct.
20, 1900; m. Pine Forge, Oct. 24, 1844, *Lemuel Allen*
(b. near Mt. Jackson, June 6, 1820; d. Mt. Jackson,
Dec. 16, 1900; p. Rhesa Allen and Catharine Kingree;
he was a farmer at "Greenwood", near Mt. Jackson,
and at San Angelo, Tex.).

    (1). FRANCIS TALIAFERRO ALLEN, b. "Green-
    wood", July 29, 1848; d. Mt. Jackson, Oct. 24,
    1872.

(2). JOSEPH RHESA ALLEN, b. "Greenwood",
Jan. 26, 1850; d. Ft. Worth, Tex., Dec. 15, 1895;
e. Roanoke College; m. Tom Green County,
Tex., Nov. 2, 1882, *Martha Frances Grooms* (b.
Key West, Fla., July 19, 1861; 1. Ft. Worth,
Texas).

    a. RHESA ALLEN, b. San Angelo, Tex., Dec.
31, 1883; d. ib. Jan. 2, 1884.

    b. IDA FRANCES ALLEN, b. ib. Jan. 18, 1885.

    c. JOSEPH STRIBLING ALLEN, b. ib. March
23, 1887.

    d. ELIZABETH JOSEPHINE ALLEN, b. ib.
March 9, 1890.

    e. ANNIE REBECCA ALLEN, b. Itaska, Tex.,
Sept. 21, 1894.

(3). LEMUEL ETHAN ALLEN, b. "Greenwood",
Oct. 10, 1852; e. Roanoke College; m. San Angelo, Tex., Dec. 8, 1880, *Minnie Annie Fisher*
(b. in Germany, Aug. 21, 1865); 1. San Angelo,
Texas.

    a. FRANK PENNYBACKER ALLEN, b. ib.
April 26, 1882.

    b. GEORGE FISHER ALLEN, b. ib. Oct. 21,
1883; d. Mansfield, Ark., Nov. 21, 1887.

    c. LEMUEL ETHAN ALLEN, b. San Angelo,
Tex., July 18, 1886.

    d. EDNA MATILDA ALLEN, b. ib. Dec. 2,
1888.

    e. RUDOLPH ROBERT ALLEN, b. ib. Nov.
28, 1891.

(4). FLORENCE WILLELMA ALLEN, b. "Greenwood", Shenandoah County, August 17, 1858;
m. Mt. Jackson, Oct. 20, 1887, *Rev. William
Elias Stahler* (b. Norristown, Pa., July 3, 1858;
he is a Lutheran minister at Lebanon, Pa.).

    a. ALAN DONALD STAHLER, b. ib. Oct. 12,
1897.

2. SARAH ANN PENNYBACKER, b. Woodstock, in
1826; d. "The White House", in May 1842.

3. CAROLINE PENNYBACKER, b. ib. in 1828; d. ib. at eighteen months of age.

§57   4. GEORGE MAYBERRY PENNYBACKER, b. ib. Feb. 2, 1830; d. Mt. Jackson, Dec. 14, 1893; m. *1st*. Richmond, July 11, 1854, *Julia Egbertine Wortham* (b. near Richmond, Oct. 31, 1834; d. Paris, Tex., Sept. 1, 1873); m. *2nd*. Baltimore, Md., Dec. 3, 1878, *Rebecca Jane Oliver* (b. ib. in 1834; l. Baltimore, Md.); he was a physician, and lived for many years at Paris and at Honey Grove, Texas, but returned to Virginia before his death.

　(1). PERCY VIVIAN PENNYBACKER, b. Paris, Tex., Feb. 17, 1856; d. Nevada, Mo., May 15, 1899; m. Tyler, Tex., Oct. 31, 1884, *Anna J. Hardwicke* (b. Petersburg, Va., May 7, 1861; l. Austin, Tex.; she is the author of a History of Texas used extensively in the schools of the State); he was Superintendent of Public Schools in Palestine, Tex.

　　a. LORINE PENNYBACKER, b. Tyler, Texas, August 18, 1885; d. ib. Jan. 6, 1886.

　　b. PAUL BONNER PENNYBACKER, b. Jefferson, Texas. April 10, 1888.

　　c. PERCY VIVIAN PENNYBACKER, b. Palestine, Texas, Jan. 7, 1895.

　　d. RUTH PENNYBACKER, b. ib. Feb. 24, 1897.

　(2). MAUD PENNYBACKER, b. Paris, Tex., Aug. 19, 1857; d. Delta County, Tex., Oct. 28, 1878.

　(3). JULIAN PENNYBACKER, b. Lamar County, Tex., March 28, 1862; m. Honey Grove, Tex., April 20, 1887, *Jennie Stephens* (b. West Station, Miss., Sept. 30, 1866); he is a wholesale book dealer at Palestine, Tex.

　　a. MAURINE EMILY PENNYBACKER, b. Honey Grove, Tex., Feb. 16, 1889; d. ib. Sept. 20, 1890.

　　b. GEORGE OLIVER PENNYBACKER, b. ib. July 15, 1892.

　　c. JULIAN WORTHAM PENNYBACKER, b. Palestine, Tex., August 16, 1895.

  d. JOE PENNYBACKER, b. ib. August 16, 1895;
    d. ib. August 20, 1895.

  e. CHARLES DANA PENNYBACKER, b. ib.
    June 19, 1897.

  f. NINA PENNYBACKER, b. ib. June 5, 1899.

(4). NINA PENNYBACKER, b. Paris, Tex., Jan.
27, 1864; d. Bonham, Tex., Jan. 12, 1897; m.
Honey Grove, Tex., Nov. 4, 1884, *Leslie Curtis
White* (b. Russellville, Ala., Feb. 23, 1861; l.
Bonham, Tex.; he is a traveling salesman).

  a. BERTINE WHITE, b. Honey Grove, Tex.,
    Oct. 16, 1885.

  b. DORIS WHITE, b. Bonham, Tex., July
    22, 1889; d. ib. Feb. 8, 1896.

  c. LESLIE GORDON WHITE, b. ib. Feb. 29,
    1892.

  d. KENNON PENNYBACKER WHITE, b. ib.
    July 20, 1893.

(5). ADELE PENNYBACKER, b. Paris, Tex., Dec.
2, 1866; m. Bonham, Tex., Oct. 10, 1888, *Benjamin Curtice Epperson* (b. New Iberia, La., Aug.
25, 1861; he is a lumber merchant at Pittsburg,
Texas).

  a. ADELE EPPERSON, b. Jefferson, Tex., Oct.
    6, 1889.

§58 5. WILLELMA TATE PENNYBACKER, b. "The White
House", April 28, 1832; d. Mt. Jackson, Feb. 6, 1861;
m. ib. Nov. 25, 1852, *Solomon Kingree Moore* (b.
Moore's Store, Shenandoah County, April 30, 1827;
d. Mt. Jackson, July 4, 1896; he lived at Mt. Jackson).

  (1). MAGNUS STRIBLING MOORE, b. ib. Feb. 21,
1855; m. *1st*. San Angelo, Tex., May 13, 1878,
Fannie Groomes of Key West, Fla.; m. *2nd*. Mt.
Jackson, May 2, 1883, *Cora Alice Ritenour* (b.
Buck Hill, Nov. 29, 1864); he is a jeweler at
Mt. Jackson; he had one child by the first mar-
riage and two by the second.

    a. FLORENCE WILLELMA MOORE, b. San An-
      gelo, Tex., Feb. 24, 1879; m. Ft. Worth,

Tex., June 24, 1897, *Samuel McHam* (b. Lamar County, Tex., Feb. 6, 1872); 1. Ft. Worth, Tex.

   (a). IRENE MCHAM, b. ib. May 14, 1898.

  b. WILLELMA GOLDIE MOORE, b. Mt. Jackson, March 24, 1885.

  c. CLARENCE ROBERT MOORE, b. ib. Sept. 16, 1888.

  (2). ARTHUR LEWIS MOORE, b. ib. Nov. 8, 1855; he is a stock dealer at Onawa, Iowa.

  (3). MARY EGBERTINE MOORE, b. Mt. Jackson, Jan. 21, 1859; d ib. March 12, 1861.

6. REBECCA JANE PENNYBACKER, b. "The White House", April 12, 1834; d. Mt. Jackson, March 21, 1881.

7. MARGARET MUSE PENNYBACKER, b. "The White House", June 12, 1836; 1. New York City.

8. JOEL PENNYBACKER, b. "The White House", Sept. 7, 1838; e. Roanoke College; d. Sioux City, Iowa, about 1876; m. St. Louis, Mo., August 8, 1866, *Eliza Marie Power* (b. Calonmel, Ireland, August 19, 1846; d. St. Louis, Mo., Feb. 6, 1900); he was a salesman.

  (1). EDWARD FRANCIS PENNYBACKER, b. ib. March 17, 1867; m. ib. Oct. 31, 1900, *Elizabeth Loretta O'Rourke* (b. ib. July 6, 1878); 1. ib.; he is chief clerk for a railroad.

    a. EDWARD RAYMOND PENNYBACKER, b. ib. Dec 8, 1901.

  (2). MADELINE PENNYBACKER, b. ib. Sept. 22, 1869; m. ib. August 1, 1896, *William Edwin Matthews* (b. Biglyville. Tenn., Jan. 31, 1870; he is a traveling salesman); 1. Memphis, Tenn.

    a. WILLIAM EDWARD MATTHEWS, b. ib. Feb. 14, 1901.

§59   9. FRANCIS STRIBLING PENNYBACKER, b. "The White House", Sept. 26, 1840; e. Roanoke College; m. "Locust Thicket", Loudoun County, Dec. 4, 1867, *Lucy Ellzey White* (b. ib. Feb. 6, 1846; see MCILHANY FAMILY, §126); he served through the Civil War in the

6th Va. Cavalry; he is now in the insurance business at Mt. Jackson.

§60 X. GEORGE WILLIAM STRIBLING, b. "Hopewell", April 9, 1802; d. Point Pleasant, W. Va., Oct. 29, 1851; m. *1st.* Mason County, W. Va., April 10, 1828, *Mary Nelson Neale* (b. Loudoun County, Sept. 10, 1802; d. Point Pleasant, W. Va., April 15, 1843; p. William Presley Neale and Nancy Maria Smith); m. *2nd.* Staunton, Dec. 8, 1845, *Mary King* (b. Norfolk, in 1812; d. Point Pleasant, W. Va., May 11, 1849); he was a lawyer, and for a number of years clerk of the circuit court of Mason County. He had four children by his first marriage and one by the second.

 1. NANNIE TATE STRIBLING, b. Point Pleasant, W. Va., March 17, 1829; d. ib. Sept. 5, 1867; m. ib. April 20, 1853, *William Smith* (b. Jan. 6, 1823; d. April 1, 1890; he was a merchant at Point Pleasant).

  (1). FRANCIS STRIBLING SMITH, b. ib. in May, 1854; l. in Connecticut; m. *Kittie Lane*, a Presbyterian minister's daughter, and had two daughters,
   a. BESSIE SMITH.
   b. NELLIE SMITH.

  (2). OLIVIA SMITH, b. Point Pleasant, W. Va., March 1, 1856; d ib. June 20, 1856.

  (3). MARY SMITH, b. ib. March 16, 1858; d. ib. March 18, 1858.

  (4). LEWIS NELSON SMITH, b. ib. April 5, 1859; d. ib. May 18, 1859.

  (5). EDGAR GARRISON SMITH, b. ib. Jan. 11, 1861; is living in Minnesota.

 2. FRANCIS STRIBLING, b. Point Pleasant, W. Va., Sept. 5, 1831; d. Staunton, Sept. 27, 1850.

 3. TALIAFERRO STRIBLING, b. Point Pleasant, W. Va , Feb. 17, 1834; d. ib. April 7, 1893; m. Hancock, Md., Dec. 4, 1862, *Mary Louise Byers* (b. Sharpsburg, Md., Jan. 9, 1835; d. Point Pleasant, W. Va., August 23, 1891; p. John A. and Charlotte M. W. Byers); he studied law at Washington College in 1853–'54; was

Cashier of the Merchants' National Bank of Point
Pleasant, W. Va.

(1). A daughter, b. and d. ib. Sept. 23, 1863.

(2). GEORGE WILLIAM STRIBLING, b. ib. Sept 2,
1864; e. West Va. University; m Elm Grove,
W. Va., June 17, 1896, *Annette Katherine Long*
(b. Mason County, W. Va., Nov. 26, 1870; p.
James W. Long and Katherine Hannan); he is
Secretary and Treasurer of the Municipal Engin-
eering and Construction Company of Baltimore.

(3). KATE BYERS STRIBLING, b. Point Pleasant,
W. Va., July 16, 1866; l. ib.

(4). NANNIE TATE STRIBLING, b. ib. Feb. 6,
1868; d. ib. Sept. 15, 1868.

(5). TALIAFERRO STRIBLING, b. ib. July 16, 1869;
e. West Va. University; he is Assistant Cashier
of the Merchants' National Bank at Point Pleasant, W. Va.

4. MATILDA JANE STRIBLING, b. ib. August 1, 1836;
d. Pleasant Flats, W. Va., July 27, 1892; m. Point
Pleasant, W. Va., April 29, 1862, *Andrew Chapman
Waggener* (b. Edgehill, W. Va., Jan. 24, 1837; p.
Col. C. B. Waggener and Margaret Lewis; gr. p. Maj.
Andrew C. Waggener and Attarah Beall—Thomas W.
Lewis and Eliza A. Beall); he is a farmer in Mason
County, W. Va.

(1). CHARLES BEALL WAGGENER, b. Point Pleasant, W. Va., March 2, 1863; d. ib. July 5, 1863.

(2). GEORGE STRIBLING WAGGENER, b. ib. July
17, 1864; d. ib. Jan. 23, 1867.

(3). LEWIS STUART WAGGENER, b. ib. Feb. 3,
1866; d. ib. Jan. 17, 1867.

(4). ANDREW CHAPMAN WAGGENER, b. ib. April
25, 1868; d. ib. Nov. 22, 1868.

(5). GRAHAM BEALL WAGGENER, b. Pleasant
Flats, W. Va., May 29, 1870; m. ib. Sept. 27,
1893, *Clara Estelle Windon* (b. Mason County,
W. Va., August 20, 1872); he is a farmer in
Mason County, W. Va.

a. Graham Windon Waggener, b. Kanawha County, W. Va., May 15, 1895.

b. Ernest Chapman Waggener, b. ib.
March 2, 1898.

c. James Samuel Waggener, b. ib. Sept.
18, 1900.

(6). Mary Susan Waggener, b. Pleasant Flats,
W. Va., Feb. 19, 1872; 1. Maggie, Mason County,
W. Va.

5. William Stark Stribling, b. Point Pleasant,
W. Va., June 8, 1847; d. ib. July 27, 1847.

---

§61 B. TALIAFERRO STRIBLING, b. Frederick County,
about 1758; was living there in 1784, but probably died shortly
afterwards unmarried, as nothing further is known of him.

---

§62 C. ANN STRIBLING, b. Frederick County, about 1760;
d. "Milton Valley", near Berryville, Jan. 15, 1811; m. "Hopewell", July 20, 1782, *John Milton*. For their more than two
hundred descendants see Milton Family, §§160–179.

---

§63 D. THOMAS STRIBLING, b. Frederick County, about
1761; d. Red House, Putnam County, W. Va., in 1821; m.
Frederick County, Dec. 4, 1788, *Elizabeth Snickers* (b. ib. Nov.
11, 1761; d. ib. April 19, 1819; for her ancestry see §§91–93).
He was a merchant at Battletown, now Berryville, and owned
a great deal of property in that neighborhood, being one of the
trustees of the town when it was established in 1798. About
1786 he made a very perilous journey to Boonsborough, Ky.,
by way of the Kanawha River and down the Ohio in a canoe,
intending to establish a trading post with the Indians, but
afterwards returned to Berryville; and about 1810 he removed
to Kanawha, West Virginia.

I. William S. Stribling, b. Berryville, in 1790; d. Mal-
den, W. Va., in 1834; he never married.

§64 II. Robert Mackey Stribling, b. Berryville, Feb. 14,
1793; d. "Mountain View", Aug. 24, 1862; graduated at
the Philadelphia Medical College; m. Fauquier County,

Jan. 29, 1818, *Caroline Matilda Clarkson* (b. ib. Feb. 8, 1800; d. "Mountain View", May 2, 1887; p. William Clarkson and Mildred Pickett); he was a physician, universally admired and beloved, and lived at "Mountain View", at Markham, Fauquier County, Va. Several of his children married descendants of Chief Justice John Marshall. See Paxton's "Marshall Family", pp. 54, 55, 99, 100, etc.

1. WILLIAM CLARKSON STRIBLING, b. "Mountain View", June 22, 1819; d. "Hartlands", in Jan. 1868; m. Columbia, Mo., *Mildred Pickett Clarkson*, his first cousin (b. "Belleview", near Warrenton; d. "Hartlands", Sept. 2, 1890; p. Henry M. Clarkson and Marion Morson Payne); he was a physician and lived at "Hartlands".

    (1). HENRY CLARKSON STRIBLING, b. ib. about 1848; d. ib. about 1851.

    (2). ROBERT MACKEY STRIBLING, b. ib. August 27, 1850; d. ib. Dec. 29, 1883.

    (3). MARION MORSON STRIBLING, b. ib. Jan. 15, 1852; m. Markham, *Dr. Walter Bruce*, who has since died; 1. Fredericksburg.

    (4). WILLIAM CLARKSON STRIBLING, b. "Hartlands", Oct. 13, 1853; m. St. Louis, Mo., Nov. 6, 1889, *Martha McKittrick* (b. ib. Jan. 12, 1866; d. ib. Nov. 5, 1892); he has recently retired from the wholesale shoe business in St. Louis, Mo.

        a. MILDRED CLARKSON STRIBLING, b. ib. August 23, 1890.

        b. WILLIAM CLARKSON STRIBLING, b. ib. Jan. 27, 1892.

    (5). ELIZABETH STRIBLING, b. "Hartlands", Feb. 14, 1855; m. ib. June 22, 1881, *John Hunton Foster* (b. The Plains, June 18, 1848; d. Marshall, Jan. 31, 1898; he was a merchant at Marshall); 1. Alexandria.

        a. THOMAS REDMON FOSTER, b. Marshall, Sept. 7, 1882.

        b. MILDRED CLARKSON FOSTER, b. ib. Oct. 11, 1886.

(6). THOMAS EDWARD STRIBLING, b. "Hartlands",July 13, 1857; m. Jacksonville, Fla., *Mary
Hart* of that place; 1. Markham.

    a. MILDRED CLARKSON STRIBLING, b. Jack-
sonville, Fla., in August, 1880; d. ib. in May,
1881.

    b. WILLIAM CLARKSON STRIBLING, b. ib. in
the winter of 1881; d. "Hartlands", June 19,
1882.

(7). JOHN SCOTT STRIBLING, b. ib. in 1860; d. ib.
Feb. 27, 1862.

(8). CAROLINE MATILDA STRIBLING, b. ib. Feb.
27, 1862; 1. Alexandria.

(9). ANNE SCOTT STRIBLING, b. "Hartlands",
March 3, 1864; d. Columbia, Mo., Feb. 28, 1887.

2. ELIZABETH SNICKERS STRIBLING, b. "Mountain
View", May 20, 1821; d. ib. in June, 1846.

§65 3. MILDRED PICKETT STRIBLING, b. "Mountain
View", Feb. 22, 1823; d. Culpeper, Dec. 1, 1898; m.
"Mountain View", Sept. 17, 1861, *John Marshall* (b.
"Leeds", Fauquier County, Oct. 9, 1822; d. "Glen-
dale", near Markham, Feb. 1, 1877; he was a gradu-
ate of Princeton, practiced law in Alexandria and
Warrenton, and after the Civil War lived at "Glen-
dale").

    (1). ROBERT STRIBLING MARSHALL, b. Fauquier
County, July 23, 1862; d. ib. April 2, 1864.

    (2). JAMES KEITH MARSHALL, b. ib. July 3, 1864;
d. ib. Dec. 16, 1880.

    (3). CAROLINE STRIBLING MARSHALL, b. "Moun-
tain View", July 30, 1866; m. ib. June 27, 1894,
Frederick Goodwin Ribble (b. Nelson County,
April 15, 1867; he is Rector of St. Stephens Episcopal Church at Culpeper).

        a. MILDRED STRIBLING MARSHALL RIBBLE,
b. Lawrenceville, April 25, 1895.

        b. FRANCES LE BARON RIBBLE, b. Wythe-
ville, August 13, 1896.

        c. FREDERICK DEANE GOODWIN RIBBLE, b.
Culpeper, Jan. 14, 1898.

d. JOHN MARSHALL RIBBLE, b. ib. May 9, 1900.

4. THOMAS STRIBLING, b. "Mountain View", Oct. 24, 1825; d. "Oakwood", in June, 1846.

5. LUCY MARSHALL STRIBLING, b. "Mountain View", Oct. 17, 1827; d. ib. in Jan. 1828.

6. ROBERT MACKEY STRIBLING (1st), b. and d. ib. March 19, 1830.

7. CAROLINE STRIBLING, b. and d. ib. March 19, 1830.

§66   8. ANNE ELIZA STRIBLING, b. ib. Jan. 14, 1832; m. ib. Feb. 28, 1855, *Withers Waller* (b. "Clifton", Stafford County, April 28, 1825; d. ib. Jan. 14, 1900; he was a farmer at "Clifton", and conducted a large herring fishery; p. Withers Waller and Katherine Conway; gr. p. William Waller and Ursula Withers); 1. "Clifton".

(1). KATHERINE HARWOOD WALLER, b. "Clifton", Jan. 24, 1857; 1. Alexandria; m. Wytheville, July 19, 1876, *Rev. Robert South Barrett* (b. Milton, N. C., June 9, 1851; d. Wytheville, Sept. 12, 1896; he was an Episcopal minister and for two years General Missioner of the Church; he had the degree of D. D.).

a. ROBERT SOUTH BARRETT, b. Richmond, March 30, 1877; m. Atlanta, Ga., Nov. 17, 1898, *Annie Viola Tupper* (b. Leavenworth, Kan., Jan. 25, 1877); he is the general representative of the Southern Railway in the City of Mexico.

(a). ROBERT TUPPER BARRETT, b. Atlanta, Ga., Jan. 8, 1900.

(b). CLIFTON WALLER BARRETT, b. Alexandria, June 1, 1901.

b. WITHERS WALLER BARRETT, b. Richmond, July 2, 1878; d. Wytheville, August 30, 1878.

c. JOHN BARKER BARRETT, b. Richmond, August 30, 1879.

d. LILA WALLER BARRETT, b. Henderson, Ky., May 10, 1881.

    e. REBECCA HARVEY BARRETT, b. ib. Oct. 7, 1883.

    f. CHARLES DODSON BARRETT, b. ib. Aug. 30, 1885.

    g. KATHERINE STEEL BARRETT, b. Atlanta, Ga., Sept. 5, 1888.

(2). CAROLINE STRIBLING WALLER, b. Falmouth, Oct. 6, 1858; d. "Mountain View", in Aug. 1859.

(3). WILLIAM CLARKSON WALLER, b. Falmouth, July 3, 1860; d. Garrisonville, in March, 1862.

(4). NANNIE WITHERS WALLER, b. "Clifton", Feb. 28, 1862; m. Clifton Chapel, Dec. 7, 1887, *Richard Cassius Lee Moncure* (b. Glencairn, near Fredericksburg, Jan. 16, 1855; he is farming near Wide Water).

    a. WITHERS WALLER MONCURE, b. ib. Sept. 25, 1889; d. Garrisonville, July 16, 1891.

    b. RICHARD CASSIUS LEE MONCURE, b. Wide Water, May 20, 1892.

    c. LOUIS AVERY MONCURE, b. ib. Feb. 12, 1894.

    d. CAROLINE CLARKSON MONCURE, b. Garrisonville, Sept. 1, 1895.

    e. VIRGINIA ANDREWS MONCURE, b. Wide Water, March 12, 1899.

(5). AGNES WALLER, b. "Clifton", Jan. 25, 1864; m. Clifton Chapel, Dec. 7, 1887, *Robert Ambler Moncure* (b. Windsor Forest, July 12, 1864; he is farming near Stafford Court House).

    a. HENRY MONCURE, b. "Fleurrys", Stafford County, March 21, 1889.

    b. JULIA WARWICK MONCURE, b. ib. May 31, 1892.

    c. ANNE ELIZA STRIBLING MONCURE, b. ib. Feb. 4, 1895.

    d. ELIZABETH ELLEN ADIE MONCURE, b. ib. Nov. 1, 1897.

    e. ROBERTA AMBLER MONCURE, b. ib. May 31, 1899.

(6). MILDRED PICKETT WALLER, b. "Clifton",
Jan. 5, 1866; 1. ib.

(7). CAROLINE STRIBLING WALLER, b. "Clifton",
Aug. 17, 1867; m. Wide Water, April 27, 1887,
John North Caldwell (b. Caldwell, W. Va., July
17, 1858; he is a farmer at Lewisburg, W. Va.).

    a. ANNE ELIZA WALLER CALDWELL, b.
Caldwell, W. Va., Jan. 18, 1888.

    b. ISABEL EAKLE CALDWELL, b. ib. March
13, 1889.

    c. JAMES ROBERTSON CALDWELL, b. ib. July
3, 1892.

    d. ROBERT DENNIS CALDWELL, b. ib. Feb. 7,
1894.

    e. CAROLINE WALLER CALDWELL, b. ib.
April 1, 1897.

    f. JOHN NORTH CALDWELL, b. ib. Feb. 24,
1899.

    g. MARTHA CALDWELL, b. Lewisburg, W.
Va., Sept. 21, 1900.

(8). MARY CARY WALLER, b. "Clifton", July 30,
1869; m. Clifton Chapel, April 27, 1893, *Alfred
Joseph Pyke* (b. Preston. England, August 23,
1865; he is farming at Wide Water).

    a. HANNAH CARR PYKE, b. "Richland",
near Wide Water, Oct. 23, 1895.

    b. ANNE STRIBLING PYKE, b. ib. Oct. 15,
1897.

    c. MARY CARY PYKE, b. "Red Top", Staf-
ford County, August 13, 1901.

(9). MARION STRIBLING WALLER, b. "Clifton",
Sept. 27, 1871; 1. ib.

(10). NELLIE LEE WALLER, b. "Clifton", Feb. 27,
1876; 1. ib.

§67   9. ROBERT MACKEY STRIBLING, b. "Mountain View",
Dec. 3, 1833; m. *1st.* "Morven", near Markham,
August 19, 1857, *Mary Cary Ambler* (b. ib. Sept. 9,
1835; d. "Mountain View", Feb. 9, 1868); m. *2nd.*
"Weyanoke", Charles City County, July 28, 1870,
Agnes Harwood Douthat (b. ib. Dec. 28, 1849); 1.

"Mountain View". He studied at the University of Virginia and at a Medical College in Philadelphia; was Colonel of a regiment of artillery during the Civil War; and has served several terms in the Virginia Legislature. He had four children by his first marriage and three by the second.

    (1). LETITIA AMBLER STRIBLING, b. near Markham, May 22, 1861; d. ib. Oct. 4, 1861.

    (2). CAROLINE STRIBLING, b. "Morven", June 17, 1863; l. "Mountain View".

    (3). THOMAS AMBLER STRIBLING, b. ib. Feb. 6, 1866; d. ib. Feb. 8, 1866.

    (4). ROBERT CARY STRIBLING, b. ib. Oct. 5, 1867; d. Newport News, April 4, 1901; he was a lawyer.

    (5). MARY DOUTHAT STRIBLING, b. "Mountain View", August 22, 1871; m. Markham, June 24, 1897, *George Howard Ford* (b. Memphis, Tenn., Oct. 25, 1871; he is teaching at the University School); l. Memphis, Tenn.

       a. AGNES HARWOOD FORD, b. ib. Jan. 14, 1899.

    (6). AGNES HARWOOD STRIBLING, b. "Mountain View", Nov. 10, 1878; d. Wide Water, in April, 1884.

    (7). WILLIAM CLARKSON STRIBLING, b. "Mountain View", April 18, 1885; l. ib.

§68   10. HENRY CLARKSON STRIBLING, b. "Mountain View", Oct. 4, 1836; m. "Leeds", June 16, 1869, *Rebecca Peyton Marshall* (b. ib. Nov. 5, 1847; d. "Clermont", Dec. 26, 1898); he is a farmer at "Clermont", near Hume, Fauquier County. He was a Lieutenant of Artillery during the Civil War.

    (1). CLAUDIA BURWELL STRIBLING, b. "Ashley", June 11, 1870; l. "Clermont".

    (2). ROBERT MACKEY STRIBLING, b. "Buck Farm", Jan. 1, 1872; d. Williamsburg, Sept. 2, 1897.

    (3). HENRY CLARKSON STRIBLING, b. "Leeds", August 20, 1874; m. Kirkwood, Mo., June 28,

1900, *Susan Amelia Lawton* of St. Louis; l. ib.,
where he is connected with the Tennent Shoe Co.

(4). JAMES KEITH MARSHALL STRIBLING, b.
"Leeds", March 20, 1877; he is a salesman in
St. Louis, Mo.

(5). GRAY CARROLL STRIBLING, b. "Leeds",
May 20, 1879; he is a salesman in St. Louis, Mo.

(6). ELIZA JAQUELIN STRIBLING, b. "Clermont",
Jan. 1, 1882; l. ib.

III. EDWARD SNICKERS STRIBLING, b. Berryville, in 1794;
d. Clarksburg, W. Va., March 9, 1818.

§69 IV. MATTHEW WRIGHT STRIBLING, b. Berryville, Oct.
16, 1796; d. Fauquier County, Sept. 25, 1845; gradu-
ated at the Philadelphia Medical College; m. Mercer's
Bottom, Mason County, W. Va., Jan. 23, 1828, *Elizabeth
Page Hereford* (b. Fauquier County, Jan. 29, 1800; d.
Atchison, Kan., Dec. 29, 1872; p. Robert Hereford and
Mary Mason Bronaugh); he lived and practiced medicine
at Point Pleasant and Charleston, W. Va.; he was in the
Virginia Legislature in 1828.

1. MARY CAROLINE STRIBLING, b. Fauquier County,
March 20, 1829; d. Atchison, Kan., Dec. 15, 1872; e.
Steubenville, Ohio; m. Marshall, Mo., March 3, 1858,
Junius Temple Hereford (b. Charleston, W. Va., in
1830; d. Atchison, Kan., Nov. 17, 1872; he was a
lawyer at Atchison).

(1). FREDERICK STRIBLING HEREFORD, b. Atchison, Kan., August 1, 1860; d. Mercer's Bottom,
W. Va., July 20, 1880.

2. MARGARET MASON STRIBLING (1st), b. Point
Pleasant, W. Va., July 10, 1830; d. Putnam County,
W. Va., Nov. 5, 1830.

3. MARGARET MASON STRIBLING (2nd), b. Charleston,
W. Va., Dec. 31, 1831; d. Mercer's Bottom, W. Va.,
August 23, 1833.

4. ROBERT MACKEY STRIBLING, b. Charleston, W.
Va., Jan. 30, 1834; d. St. Louis, Mo., Jan. 30,
1888; e. Drenen College, Ky., and graduated at the
Ohio Medical College, Cincinnati. He was a surgeon

in the Confederate Army, and after the War practiced
in St. Louis. He never married.

5.　OTIS FRANCIS STRIBLING, b. Point Pleasant, W. Va.,
Sept. 13, 1836; e. Gallipolis, Ohio, and at the Lexington Law School, Va., now the Law Department of
Washington & Lee University; m. Ben Lomond, W.
Va., Nov. 9, 1869, *Virginia Caroline Neale* (b. ib. Nov.
24, 1839; p. Wm. P. Neale and Catherine Steenbergen;
gr. p. Wm. Neale and Ann Smith, of Loudoun County.—Peter H. Steenbergen and Maria Jourdan); he
is a farmer at Mercer's Bottom, Mason County, W. Va.

(1).　MATTHEW WEIGHTMAN STRIBLING, b. ib.
Jan. 13, 1871; m. Point Pleasant, W. Va., Dec.
29, 1897, *Mary Margaret Hunter* (b. Ironton,
Ohio, Oct. 3, 1873); he is a farmer at Mercer's
Bottom, W. Va.

(2).　CATHERINE BEALE STRIBLING, b. ib. March
13, 1873; m. Huntington, W. Va., Dec. 26, 1899,
James Albert Young (b. Magnolia, Ark., April
5, 1870; he is an insurance agent at Nashville,
Tenn.).

(3).　ELIZABETH VIRGINIA CAROLINE STRIBLING,
b. Mercer's Bottom, W. Va., August 18, 1875;
d. ib. March 26, 1902.

(4).　WILLIAM NEALE STRIBLING, b. ib. Dec. 13,
1877; l. ib.

---

§70 E.　WILLIAM STRIBLING, b. Frederick County, about
1763; d. ib. in the early part of 1793; m. ib. April 23, 1789, *Mrs.
Sarah Berry-Humphreys*, widow of John Humphreys (who in
his will, made July 8, 1775, approved March 4, 1777, mentions his wife, Sarah Humphreys, and her father Benjamin Berry, but no children), and daughter of Benjamin Berry of Berryville (who in deeds mentions his daughter Sarah Stribling and
his grand-daughter Elizabeth T. Stribling). It is recorded in
April, 1783, that William Stribling, orphan of Taliaferro Stribling, dec'd, chose Francis Stribling as his guardian. He was
a merchant in Winchester, and at his early death left property
valued at more than $8000.00. His wife must have been sev-

eral years his senior, and she lived to an old age, dying in Butler County, Ky., in 1827. It was partly on her land that Berry-ville was established Jan. 15, 1798. In her will, a copy of which is on record in the Frederick court house, she mentions her two daughters.

    I. ELIZABETH T. STRIBLING, b. Winchester, about 1790; m. June 14, 1810, *George Steptoe Lane*. They had four children.

        1. MARY LANE, m. *Marshall Nicklin*. She left no children.

        2. ELIZABETH LANE, m. *Fisher Ames Lewis* of ''The Rocks''; see §88. She lived only two years after marriage, and left no children.

        3. JOSEPH LANE, died unmarried.

        4. BENJAMIN LANE, died unmarried.

    II. DULCIBELLA W. STRIBLING, b. Winchester about 1792; m. after 1815, *Edward Beeson*, and moved to Texas, leaving several children at her death.

------

§71 F. JOHN STRIBLING, b. Frederick County, about 1765; d. ib. about 1797; m. ib. January 20, 1792, *Sarah Drummond*, an only child of one John Drummond. After his death she married July 8, 1802, Alexander Ross Milton (see MILTON FAMILY, §146). He had two children.

    I. BUSHROD STRIBLING, b. Frederick County, Sept. 16, 1794; d. ib. unmarried August 18, 1824.

    II. JOHN STRIBLING, b. ib Oct. 11, 1796; d. ib. May 5, 1806.

§72. **Thomas Stribling,** the progenitor of the South
Carolina branch of the family, was undoubtedly the son of
Thomas and Elizabeth Taliaferro Stribling (see §22). While I
have no positive proof of this connection. the following facts seem
to indicate its certainty. Mr. J. W. Stribling of Seneca, S. C.,
writes that he has been unable to trace his ancestors further back
than to Thomas Stribling who emigrated from Berryville, Va., to
Union County, S. C. The uniform tradition among the family
of Rear Admiral Cornelius Stribling has been that this Thomas
Stribling, said to have been of Swedish and Welsh descent (?),
"left Berryville, then Battletown, when quite young, his father
giving him a horse, gun and colored man, with which to seek his
fortune in the world"; and that he finally settled in South Carolina. Dr. S. S. Neill (§ 51), who was always considered an au-
thority in such matters, wrote some years before his death that
Taliaferro Stribling (§23), though he did not know that this was
his name, had a brother who came with him and his father from
Prince William County to Frederick County, and who afterwards
removed to South Carolina and became the ancestor of the Striblings of that State. One thing is certain, that the members of
the two branches who have been acquainted have always claimed
a close kinship with one another.

§73.   It can be safely said, therefore, that Thomas Stribling,
born in Prince William County about 1730, moved first to Frederick County and thence, shortly after 1750, to South Carolina,
where he settled on Seneca River in what is now Anderson County. He afterwards married *Nancy Kincheloe,* said to have been
of English and Irish parentage. She may have been a sister or
a daughter of Cornelius Kincheloe (son of John Kincheloe), who
was Surveyor of Prince William County in 1768; for his name occurs frequently among her descendants. They had a family of
at least four children,—Thomas, Jesse, Lucy (m. ——— Trimmier), and Nancy (m. ——— Tate). There was perhaps a fifth
child, Sigismund, whose son John B. Stribling moved from South
Carolina to Tennessee in 1834, and was the ancestor of Striblings
now living at Clifton, Lawrenceburg and other places in that
State. A history of Tennessee published in 1886 states that this

John B. Stribling was "an own cousin of Commodore Cornelius
K. Stribling". The names Sigismund, Casimir and Kincheloe
occur in this branch of the family, indicating the connection with
the other branches.

Because of lack of time I have not attempted to trace the
descendants of Thomas and Nancy Stribling in detail, and for
the following outline of the families of their two sons Thomas
and Jesse I am indebted almost entirely to Mr. C. K. Stribling
(§75) of Fort Griffin, Texas, and to Miss Mary Stribling (§82)
of Walhalla, S. C. These facts are given without verification on
my part with the hope that they may some time be used as the
basis of a more extended history of that branch of the family.

§74. A. THOMAS STRIBLING married *Elizabeth Haile* of
South Carolina, daughter of John Haile and Ruth Mitchell.
They had seven children.

   I. ROBERT STRIBLING, m. *Sabra Clark.* He moved with
   his family from Georgia to Arkansas.

   II. MARK MITCHELL STRIBLING, married and had five
   sons (Flavius Josephus, Harrison, Oliver, Matthew and
   Robert) and several daughters, with whom he moved
   from Pickens County, Ala., to Mississippi about 1836.

   III. BENJAMIN HAILE STRIBLING, m. Nov. 21, 1820,
   Ruth Bradley Greenwood: issue,—

      1. JAMES HARRISON STRIBLING, D. D., for fifty years
      a prominent Baptist minister in Texas. He married
      Jane Cleveland, a grand-daughter of Nancy Stribling–
      Tate (§73): issue,—Kate (m. Ad. Gentry), Ruth (m.
      Hugh Witcher), Fannie (m. —— Morrison), Cleve-
      land, and Cornelius K. Some of them are living at
      Rockdale, Tex.

      2. MARIA ELIZABETH STRIBLING, m. *William Mills
      Tandy:* issue,—James A., Ben, Frank, Mary Jose-
      phine, Cordelia, Ruth, Kate and William.

      3. THOMAS H. STRIBLING, a lawyer and for many years
      District Judge; m. *Eleanor Alexander:* issue,—Lola,
      Elizabeth (m. Price Maury of Charlottesville, Va.;
      five children), and Ben (1. San Antonio, Texas).

      4. BENJAMIN F. STRIBLING, m. *Effie McNeal:* issue,—
      Cornelius K., Frank, Clem, Kitty and Benjamin.

§75   5. CORNELIUS KINCHELOE STRIBLING, b. Feb. 28, 1833; m. *Nancy C. Stribling* (see §82).   He is county surveyor at Fort Griffin, Texas.

(1). CALLIE RUTH STRIBLING, m. *John Bennett:* issue,—Merle, Neil Clinton, Stephen, Omie, Callie, John.

(2). OLLIE PICKENS STRIBLING, m. *Woodson Coffee:* issue,—Ben Stribling, Woodson, Oran, Roy Coburn, Ollie.

(3). BEN DAVID STRIBLING, m. *Sue Graham:* issue,—David, Albert, Susie.

(4). JOE NAN STRIBLING, m. *Samuel Stewart:* issue,—Ida, Charles, C. K.

(5). MARY ELIZABETH STRIBLING, m. *Robert B. Robertson:* issue,—George.

(6). IDA ELLEN STRIBLING.

(7). FRANK BENNETT STRIBLING.

(8). FREDERICK HODGES STRIBLING.

6. MOLLIE FRANCIS STRIBLING, m. *F. C. Kelly:* issue, —Bird and Cora.

7. NANCY A. STRIBLING, m. *William H. Gentry:* issue, —George, Henry and Bruce.

8. EMILY STRIBLING, m. *Maj. L. M. Rogers:* issue,— Willie, Gentry and Nettie.

9. WILLIAM H. C. STRIBLING, m. *Allie Kesee:* issue,— Frank, Nannie and Emily.

§76 IV. CORNELIUS KINCHELOE STRIBLING, b. in 1796; m. in 1820, *Helen Maria Payne* (p. Benjamin Payne and Mary Maxwell; gr. p. Capt. Maxwell and Helen Calvert; gr. gr. p. Maximilian Calvert; gr. gr. gr. p. Cornelius Calvert and Mary Saunders; gr. gr. gr. gr. p. Rev. Jonathan and Mary Saunders).   He was appointed a midshipman in the U. S. Navy June 18, 1812; promoted to Lieutenant April 1, 1818; Commander March 11, 1840; Captain August 1, 1853; appointed to command East India Squadron April 29, 1859; Commodore August 2, 1862; Rear Admiral on the Retired List, August 6, 1866; d. Martinsburg, W. Va., Jan. 17, 1880.

1. ELIZABETH STRIBLING, d. unmarried.

2. LOUISA STRIBLING, d. unmarried.

REAR-ADMIRAL CORNELIUS K. STRIBLING
76

3. MARY STRIBLING, d. unmarried.
4. CORNELIUS KINCHELOE STRIBLING, b in 1831; m. *1st.* in 1852, *Emma J. Nourse*; m. *2nd.* in 1863, *Ann Elizabeth Riddle.* He had two children by the first marriage and five by the second.

> (1). CORNELIUS K. STRIBLING, m. *Mamie McDanald;* issue,—Mamie, Helen and Cornelius.
>
> (2). LOUISA PAYNE STRIBLING, m. *William H. Criswell:* issue,—Emma Nourse and William H.
>
> (3). CHARLES RIDDLE STRIBLING, m. *Janie B. Armstrong:* issue,—A. Elizabeth, Agnes Brown, Charles R., and Janie B. He is pastor of the Presbyterian Church at Waynesboro, Va.
>
> (4). JOHN M. STRIBLING, d. in 1866.
>
> (5). JAMES MAXWELL STRIBLING.
>
> (6). MARY CALVERT STRIBLING.
>
> (7). SUE BROWN STRIBLING, m. *Magnus A. Snodgrass:* issue,—Ann Porterfield and Cornelius Stribling.

5. JOHN MAXWELL STRIBLING. He was a Lieutenant in the U. S. Navy; resigned in Feb. 1861 to serve in the C. S. Navy with Admiral Semmes. He ran the blockade at Mobile, Sept. 10, 1862, and died of yellow fever a few days later, aged 27.

V. MARY STRIBLING, m. *Richard Roseman* or *Rosamond.* They had a large family and moved to Mississippi.

VI. FRANCES STRIBLING, m. *I. J. Foster;* moved from Union District, S. C., in 1847, to Lavacca, Texas: issue,—A. K., Thompson, Haile, Benton, Clem, Sarah and Frances.

VII. MARIA STRIBLING, m——— *Moreland;* moved to Arkansas.

§77 B. JESSE STRIBLING, b. April 9, 1775; d. Nov. 30, 1841; m. April 29, 1805, *Elizabeth Sloan*, daughter of David Sloan (b. in 1751; d. Oct. 9, 1826) and Susan Majors (b. July 29, 1763; d. Sept. 5, 1854).

I. THOMAS M. STRIBLING, b. Jan. 25, 1806; d. Dec. 31, 1879; m. *Mary Jones* (b. May 3, 1813; d. Nov. 9, 1867).

1. JONES H. STRIBLING, b. June 23, 1834; d. July 7, 1862, in the Confederate Army.

2. WILLIAM E. STRIBLING, b. July 6, 1837; d. July 6, 1862, in the Confederate Army.

3. THOMAS JABES STRIBLING, b. July 13, 1839; killed in the Confederate Army, April 25, 1865.

4. MARTHA HANNAH STRIBLING, b. July 1, 1841; m. *Alexander Ramsey;* 1. Seneca, S. C.

    (1). ELIZABETH RAMSEY, b. in May, 1864; 1. Seneca, S. C.; m. *Yancey Sligh:* issue,—Harry Kuthman, b. in April, 1892, and Edgar Yancey, b. in Dec. 1896.

    (2). SALLIE R. RAMSEY, b. June 1866; 1. Anderson, S. C.; m. *Townes Holleman:* issue,—J. Ramsey, b. August 1889; Frank A., b. Nov. 1891; Whitfield, b. June 1894; Julian Bruce, b. June 1897, and Sarah Lee, b. May 1899.

    (3). W. ALEXANDER RAMSEY, b. August 1869; m. *Clelia Lowery:* issue,—Gladys, b. April 1893; 1. Ellesville, Miss.

    (4). EUGENE BASKIN RAMSEY, b. Oct. 1873; m. *Lula Lawrence*: issue,—Lilian, b. Nov. 1898; Mattie E , b. Feb. 1901; 1. Seneca, S. C.

    (5). THOMAS R. RAMSEY, b. May 1880; m. *Susan Kennimore:* issue,—Martha E., b. Dec. 1900; Linda K., b. July 1902.

5. JESSE CORNELIUS STRIBLING, b. Sept. 27, 1844; m. June 5, 1867, *Virginia Hunter;* 1. Pendleton, S. C.

    (1). HARRY LEE STRIBLING, b. Nov. 20, 1869; m. May 4, 1892, *Ella Osborne:* issue,—Augustus Lee, b. Jan. 30, 1893; Raymond Wilson, b. Jan. 23, 1895; Robert, b. Sept. 13, 1899.

    (2). JESSE CORNELIUS STRIBLING, b. Oct. 25, 1876; m. Feb. 18, 1902, *Meta Henshael*.

    (3). JAMES HUNTER STRIBLING, b. Dec. 19, 1878.

    (4). MARY ELIZA STRIBLING, b. May 19, 1881.

    (5). THOMAS EUGENE STRIBLING, b. August 23, 1883; d. August 4, 1894.

    (6). ELIZABETH STRIBLING, b. August 14, 1885.

    (7). ROXIE ALICE STRIBLING, b. March 14, 1887.

§78   6. MARY E. STRIBLING, b. July 31, 1846; m. Jan. 20,
1870, *Clayton Lytle Reid* (b. Sept. 25, 1838).   He first
married her sister; see below.

(1). CHARLES SLOAN REID, b. April 30, 1871; m.
Dec. 4,1897, *Louise Strother:* issue,—Frances Elizabeth, b. Sept, 24, 1898; Roxie Louise, b. Sept.
28, 1901; l. Walhalla, S. C.

(2). ROXIE ELIZABETH REID, b. Dec. 15, 1872;
l. Walhalla, S. C.

(3). CLAYTON JONES REID, b. Feb. 10, 1874; d.
July 7, 1874.

(4). J. B. SITTON REID, b. Oct. 8, 1876.

(5). MARY ANNIE REID, b. Dec. 17, 1878.

(6). SARAH ELLA REID, b. July 8, 1881.

7. SLOAN Y. STRIBLING, b. Dec. 18, 1848; m. Dec. 1,
1871, *Ida Sligh* (b. Oct. 12, 1853); l. Roswell, Ga.; is
president of a cotton mill.

(1). THOMAS SLIGH STRIBLING, b. Oct. 31, 1872;
m. Nov. 29, 1899, *Julia Maude Verner:* issue,—
Mary Ida, b. Nov. 16, 1900; Robert Sloan, b.
Nov. 10, 1901.

(2). PAUL ORLANDO STRIBLING, b. June 18, 1874;
m. Nov. 30, 1899, *Yancy Jane Bush:* issue,—Paul
Orlando, b. Oct. 11, 1900; Dorothy, b. Dec. 24,
1901.

(3). MARY KATHERINE STRIBLING, b. Dec. 25,
1876; l. Roswell, Ga.

(4). JONES HOUCK STRIBLING, b. August 18, 1879.

(5). EARLE STRIBLING, b. July 29, 1882.

(6). NINA SLOAN STRIBLING, b. June 10, 1885.

(7). MARTHA NEEL STRIBLING, b. July 12, 1888.

(8). SUMMER YOWELL STRIBLING, b. Feb. 16,
1891.

(9). HUGH YANCY STRIBLING, b. Oct. 10, 1893.

8. ROXIE A. STRIBLING, b. May 27, 1850; d. April 24,
1869; m. March 12, 1868, *Clayton Lytle Reid* (b. Sept.
25, 1838).   He afterwards married her sister; see above.

(1). THOMAS CLAYTON REID, b. March 8, 1869;
d. July 15, 1869.

9. LLEWELLEN STRIBLING, b. Oct. 25, 1853; d. Jan. 25, 1902; m. *Mrs. Ida D. Fincannon.*
    (1). CLIFTON EARLE STRIBLING, b. July, 1877.
    (2). MARY E. STRIBLING, b. Oct., 1879.
    (3). STELLA AMELIA STRIBLING, b. Sep. 23, 1881.
    (4). ELIZABETH ETHEL STRIBLING, b. March, 1885.

II. MARY S. STRIBLING, b. June 4, 1807; m. *Hartwell Jones.* They had thirteen children.

§79 III. WILLIAM HARRISON STRIBLING, b. Feb. 9, 1809; d. Nov. 23, 1889; m. Sept. 27, 1832, *Jane B. McKindly* (b. Dec. 23, 1815; d. Oct. 3, 1855).

1. JESSE SLOAN STRIBLING, b. August 5, 1833; d. June 27, 1856.

2. ELIZABETH CAROLINE STRIBLING, b. Dec. 18, 1835; 1. Seneca, S. C.; m. Jan. 4, 1866, *James T. Reid.*
    (1). ELIZABETH REID, b. Nov. 24, 1866; 1. Washington, D. C.; m. Dec. 6, 1887, *James M. Webb:* issue,—James R., b. Nov. 9, 1889; William C., b. May 5, 1892.
    (2). SAMUEL REID, b. July 19, 1869; m. Feb. 2, 1898, *Myra Lay:* issue,—James S., b. Nov. 2, 1898; Mamie J., b. June 28, 1900.
    (3). GEORGE T. REID, b. March 13, 1871; m. March 10, 1892, *Jane Fisher:* issue,—Ludie C., b. May 21, 1893; William R., b. Nov. 15, 1894; E. Caroline, b. July 2, 1896; George Braxton, b. April 7, 1898; Frank, b. Jan. 3, 1900; Samuel, b. Oct. 27, 1901.
    (4). MAMIE REID, b. Sept. 26, 1874; m. July 20, 1898, *Dr. W. Frank Ashmore:* issue,—Elizabeth C., b. March 30, 1901; 1. Newry, S. C.

3. THOMAS H. STRIBLING, b. May 23, 1838, m. Sept. 3, 1867, *Josie Reeder* (b. January 14, 1846); is farming in Oconee County, S. C.
    (1). ESSIE S. STRIBLING, b. Jan. 26, 1870; d. Oct. 2, 1870.
    (2). SUE ALICE STRIBLING, b. in 1871; m. Feb. 8, 1893, *John Lawrence:* issue,—Thomas Charles, b. Feb. 1, 1894; Mattie Louise, b. Feb. 17, 1896;

Jesse Stribling, b. Sept. 30, 1897; John, b. Sept. 8, 1899; Joe, b. April 29, 1902; d. July 31, 1902; l. Seneca, S. C.

    (3). WILLIAM H. STRIBLING, b. May 19, 1874.

    (4). JESSIE S. STRIBLING, b. Jan. 1, 1878.

4. MARY ELIZA STRIBLING, b. Dec. 23, 1840; d. May 1, 1889; m. Dec. 6, 1860, *William A. Barron* (d. March 30, 1887).

    (1). IDA BARRON, b. Sept. 11, 1861; l. Seneca, S. C.; m. Oct. 16, 1883, *Lawrence McMahan*.

    (2.) WILLIE BARRON, b. in 1866; d August 17, 1901; m. August 15, 1889, *Nan Bibbs*.

    (3.) SALLIE BARRON, b. in 1868; d. March 7, 1895; m. Dec. 22, 1891, —— *McMahan*.

    (4). ROSA BARRON, b. Jan. 8, 1871.

    (5). ELIJAH MACK BARRON, b. July 1, 1873; m. Dec. 26, 1897, *Belle Biggerstaff;* l. Seneca, S. C.

    (6). MAMIE BARRON, b. Dec. 12, 1875.

    (7). E. STOKES BARRON, b. May 5, 1878; m. Dec. 22, 1896, *J. F. Alexander*.

§80   5. JAMES McB. STRIBLING, b. July 13, 1843; killed at the battle of Fredericksburg, Dec. 13, 1862.

6. WILLIAM DAVID STRIBLING, b. Nov. 10, 1845; m. *Louise Harbin:* issue,—Ora Jane, Samuel S., Carrie May, Hattie K., Robert Warren; l. Richland, S. C.

7. ELIJAH S. STRIBLING, b. April 25, 1848; d. June 4, 1865.

8. ROBERT W. STRIBLING, b. April 9, 1851; d. July 7, 1869.

9. SUSAN J. STRIBLING, b. Sept. 5, 1854; l. Richland, S. C.; m. Dec. 22, 1869, *Orwed Sligh*.

    (1). ROBERT CLARENCE SLIGH, b. Oct. 10, 1870; m. June 30, 1893, *Daisy A. Bobbitt:* issue,—Roy Clair, b. August 1894; d. August 1895; Glenn Orr, b. Feb. 23, 1896.

    (2). SARAH KATE SLIGH, b. Sept. 2, 1872; d. Oct. 8, 1896; m. August 31, 1894, *E. B. Smith*.

    (3). ROWENNE FAY SLIGH, b. Oct. 19, 1874; d. Jan. 31, 1893.

(4). NEEL SLIGH, b. Oct. 2, 1876; m. June 30, 1901, *Emma C. Gaines.*

(5). SUE SLIGH, b. Oct. 12, 1878; m. Dec. 10, 1899, *Frank Patterson:* issue,—Neel, b. April 20, 1901.

IV. REBECCA C. STRIBLING, b. Sept. 10, 1810, m. *B. F. Kilpatrick;* they lived in Mississippi.

V. ROBERT STRIBLING, b. March 12, 1812; d May 11, 1877; m.Jan. 30, 1834, *Ruth P. Bruce:* issue,—Susan E., b. 1834; d. 1837; Mary C., b. 1836; d. 1844; Susan Annie, b. 1839; d. 1843; Robert, b. 1841; died during the War; Thomas W., b. 1844; d. 1852.

§81 VI. DAVID SLOAN STRIBLING, b. July 3, 1814; d. Sept. 13, 1883; m. Oct. 16, 1834, *Jo Anna C. Hodges* (b. Nov. 18, 1814; p. James and Elizabeth Brown Hodges).

1. MARY E. STRIBLING, b. Dec. 23, 1835; 1. Acton, Tex.; m. *Larkin C. Cleveland.*

(1). LOU BERRY CLEVELAND.

(2). ESSIE W. CLEVELAND, m. *Edward Clifton:* issue,—Claude, Joseph Earle.

(3). ANNIE J. CLEVELAND, m. *Clifton Davis:* issue,—Trenholm.

(4). HASKELL O. CLEVELAND.

(5). CARLTON CLEVELAND.

2. JESSE WALES STRIBLING, b. April 28, 1838; m. *1st.* Nov. 9, 1859, *Sarah Shelor* (b. Sept. 18, 1837; she was his first cousin; see §83); m. *2nd.* Sept. 1889, *Mrs. Sallie C. Cherry;* 1. Seneca, S. C.; he is cashier of a bank.

(1). THOMAS EDWARD STRIBLING, b. August 27, 1860; m. *Mattie Verner:* issue,—Thomas Edward, Verner, Jesse W., Charles; 1. Seneca, S. C.

(2). EMMA P. STRIBLING, b. July 17, 1863.

(3). JO ANNA STRIBLING, b. Oct. 17, 1867; d. July 29, 1900; m. Dec. 28, 1887, *Thomas M. Lowery:* issue,—Wales, b. Feb. 17, 1889; Thomas M., Sarah, Louise Emma.

3. LUCINDA W. STRIBLING, b. Oct. 4, 1840; d. Aug. 6, 1887; m. *Dr. John N. Doyle;* 1. Granbury, Tex.

(1). MAMIE B. DOYLE.

(2). ROBERT EDWARD DOYLE, m. Dec. 25, 1900,
Bessie ———: issue,—Robert Edward; 1. Granbury, Tex.

(3). HATTIE B. DOYLE.

4. RUTH P. STRIBLING, b. Jan. 14, 1843; d. Dec. 2, 1867.

§82   5. NANCY C. STRIBLING, b. July 10, 1845; m. *Cornelius K. Stribling;* see §75.

6. REBECCA C. STRIBLING, b. June 10, 1847; d. Sept. 12, 1875; m. *James A. Tandy.*

    (1). EMMET TANDY.

    (2). JOHN CLARK TANDY, m. *Josie Kerr:* issue,—Madeline; 1. Granbury, Tex.

    (3). DAVID SLOAN TANDY, m. *Maud Donathan:* issue,—Fay, Flo.

7. JAMES HODGES STRIBLING, b. April 4, 1849; m. *Zena Taylor:* issue,—Lillie Maude (m. *Ben Clifton:* issue,—Kathleen), Jesse, Bessie Lee, Ethel, Fred H., Myrtle, Warren, James Oran; 1. Acton, Tex.

8. WILLIAM JOHN STRIBLING, b. May 12, 1851; m. Dec. 15, 1880, *Lizzie Norton* (b. Feb. 15, 1861; p. Joseph J. Norton and Tabitha A. Campbell); issue,—Mary, b. March 6, 1882; Sallie, b. July 9, 1886; Anna, b. June 26, 1888; Frances, b. Dec. 15, 1890; Norton, b. Sept. 6, 1892; Elizabeth, b. Nov. 26, 1894; Tabitha Atkinson, b. Oct. 30, 1898; William John, b. Aug. 12, 1901; 1. Walhalla, S. C.; he is a lawyer.

9. LUCY C. STRIBLING, b. June 21, 1853; m. *James A. Tandy:* issue,—Burt E. (1. Blanket, Texas), Mary Viola (m. Dec. 1900, ——— *Jarrett*), Albert, Elizabeth, Lou, Lucy; 1. Acton, Tex.

§83 VII. SUSAN A. STRIBLING, b. Jan. 22, 1817; m. *Thomas R. Shelor.*

1. MARY SHELOR, m. *Dr. Harbin:* issue,—Thomas (m. *Ida Harland:* issue,—Maxwell, Milda; 1. Calhoun, Ga.); Dr. Robert M. (m. *Jane Acker;* 1. Rome, Ga.); Dr. William (1. Rome, Ga.); Nina.

2. SARAH E. SHELOR, m. *Jesse W. Stribling;* see §81. She was his first cousin.

3.   REBECCA SHELOR, 1. Calhoun, Ga.; m. *William Steele:* issue,—Annie (m. William Swain; four children); Virginia (m.———Garet; issue,—Robert, Bertha); Thomas; Henry; Sadah (m. Dr. Franklin: issue, Minerva); Robert.

4.   VIRGINIA SHELOR, 1. Calhoun, Ga.; m. *Calvin Wright:* issue,—Sunie, C. Shelor, Jesse, Frederick.

5.   JESSE R. SHELOR, m. *Emma Bruce:* issue,—J. Wales, Mamie, Ryland, Clarence, Floy, Varina.

6.   JOSEPH W. SHELOR, m. *1st.* Nov. 7, 1878, *Lou Neville*; m. *2nd.* Feb. 27, 1883, *Lizzie Hix:* issue,—Sallie, b. May 12, 1880; Hattie, b. August 11, 1884; T. B., b. Dec. 7, 1890; 1. Calhoun, Ga.

7.   WILLIAM SHELOR, m. *Ada Swain:* issue,—Mary, Sudie, Louise, Swain, Ellen, Ethel, Joe, William C.; 1. Calhoun, Ga.

8.   SUSAN SHELOR, m. *Dr. G. W. Gardner;* 1. Greenwood, S. C.

§84 VIII.   M. STOKES STRIBLING, b. May 2, 1819; d. 1890; m. May 2, 1843, *Anna M. Verner* (d. March 4, 1901).

1.   REBECCA E. STRIBLING, b. Dec. 16, 1843; d. Sept. 6, 1877; m. June 10, 1867, *Warren Shelor:* issue,—Toccoa, Stokes W. (m. Dec. 27, 1901, *Mrs. A. Duckett*); 1. Seneca, S. C.

2.   LEMUEL DAVID STRIBLING, b. March 1, 1845; m. Nov. 26, 1867, *Martha Jane Brownlee:* issue,—Annie, Talula Kate, Clinton, Mary, Rebecca, George Brownlee, Joseph Clark, Jesse D., Maria Perry, Montford, Mattie E.; 1. Helena, Ga.

3.   JOHN VERNER STRIBLING, b. Jan. 30, 1847; m. Dec. 23, 1875, *Susan Willard*: issue,—Annie Verner (m. in 1900, *Joe Jenings:* issue,—Willard; 1. Anderson, S. C.), Samuel, William George, James Wyatt, John Carl, Carrie; 1. Anderson, S. C.; he is a civil engineer.

4.   WILLIAM JESSE STRIBLING, b. May 25, 1848; m. Nov. 26, 1873, *Augusta Jamison:* issue,—Effie Young, Jessie Rebecca, Leo, Maude, Allie Marie, Roy, Jamison, Grace Augusta, Frank; 1. Westminster, S. C.; he is a merchant.

5. SAMUEL PETTIGREW STRIBLING, b. Feb. 11, 1850; m. Nov. 27, 1875, *Jane Sheldon:* issue,—Margaret Hampton, Leslie, Mark; 1. Fair Play, S. C.

6. GEORGE THOMAS STRIBLING, b. July 9, 1851; m. *Hattie West.* issue,—Garnet, B. B., Eugene, Myrtle, Lillian; 1. Atlanta, Ga.; he is a travelling salesman.

7. MARY JANE STRIBLING, b. Dec. 31, 1852; m. May 7, 1874, *John W. Shelor:* issue,—Marye, Rebecca, Annie, Wayne, Ryland, Gama, Jane, George; 1. Tugaloo, S. C.

8. SUSAN M. STRIBLING, b. Sept 18, 1854.

9. ANNIE MARIA STRIBLING, b. Oct. 5, 1856; 1. Richland, S. C.; m. June 11, 1878, *Thomas B. Wyly:* issue,—Byrd Samuel, Stokes Oliver, Anna Adaline, David Lemuel, Jamie D., Cora R., Clark J., Hugh Strong, Lola, Lula, Wayne.

10. M. STOKES STRIBLING, b. April 19, 1859; m. in 1880, *Elizabeth Brown:* issue,—Elizabeth, Mary; 1. Seneca, S. C.; is a commission merchant.

11. WARREN D. STRIBLING, b. Nov. 16, 1860; m. in 1888, *Alice Butler:* issue,—Mayfield, Samuel, Eliza, Edwin Warren, Faith; 1. Eatonton, Ga.

12. EBENEZER SLOAN STRIBLING, b. April 7, 1862; 1. Eatonton, Ga.

13. JOSEPH SHELOR STRIBLING, b. Jan. 10, 1864; is a physician at Seneca, S. C.

§85 IX. NANCY TRIMMIER STRIBLING, b. August 7, 1821; d. Feb. 20, 1887; m. Oct. 11, 1838, *Henry N. White* (b. Sept. 2, 1812; d. Jan. 13, 1884).

1. B. FRANK WHITE, b. March 31, 1849; married three times; issue,—Monroe, William, Birdie, and others; 1. Greenville, S. C.

2. D. SLOAN WHITE, b. Nov. 3, 1852; m. Oct. 30, 1872, *Virginia Cox:* issue,—Iola Pearl, b. August 11, 1873 (m. W. E. Ledbetter); Kiturah Gertrude, b. Nov. 21, 1875 (m. E. M. Sturges); Latula Trimmier, b. March 22, 1878 (m. Fred. R. Young); Bonner Sloan, b. July 22, 1880; Clarence Stokes, b. March 6, 1883; Henry Lucius, b. August 13, 1885; Allie Mira, b. Sept. 25, 1888; Horace Hodges, b. June 27, 1893; d. March 26, 1894; 1. Sherman, Tex.

3. SALLIE E. WHITE, b. Jan. 21, 1855.

X. ELIZABETH KATHERINE STRIBLING, b. Nov. 27, 1823; d. July 26, 1860; m. Nov. 14, 1852, *Josiah Harkey* (b. in April 1818; d. March 2, 1863): issue,—Joseph F., Mary E., Susan E., Henry Bass, William C.; (l. Atlanta, Ga.).

§86 XI. WARREN WEBB STRIBLING, b. April 18, 1826; d. Dec. 14, 1872; m. Dec. 11, 1850, *Emily Rebecca Dendy* (b. June 5, 1831).

    1. ELIZABETH CATHERINE STRIBLING, b. Oct. 26, 1851; m. Oct. 14, 1874, *Sloan Bruce:* issue,—Minerva Emily, b. June 29, 1875; d. Oct. 4, 1885; l. Richland, S. C.

    2. MARSHALL STOKES STRIBLING, b. Jan. 24, 1854; m. Dec. 22, 1886, *Martha Helen Sheldon:* issue,—Margie, b. August 29, 1887; Lee Webb, b. June 24, 1890; Alice, b. August 6, 1894; Emily, b. August 29, 1897; l. Seneca, S. C.

    3. ROBERT STILES STRIBLING, b. Nov. 2, 1856; d. June 29, 1879.

    4. LOU ALICE STRIBLING, b. Oct. 22, 1859; m. Aug. 28, 1889, *John Newton Doyle:* issue,—Lucy Stribling, b. June 22, 1890; d. Dec. 28, 1894; Emily, b. June 5, 1894.

    5. JAMES PAUL STRIBLING, b. July 19, 1862; m. Dec. 10, 1891, *Bessie May Conger:* issue,—Edna, b. Sept. 4, 1892; d. Sept. 7, 1896; Stiles Conger, b. May 21, 1894; Bruce Hodgson, b. Jan. 16, 1896; Belle Bernice, b. Dec. 16, 1897; Charles Lane, b. March 10, 1899; d. June 29, 1901; James Paul, b. April 30, 1902; l. Richland, S. C.

    6. THOMAS MCKNIGHT STRIBLING, b. Nov. 30, 1865; l. Princeton College.

    7. LUCY TRIMMIER STRIBLING, b. April 6, 1868; l. Greenville, S. C.; m. Oct. 17, 1894, *Green Berry Jordan:* issue,—Emily, b. June 5, 1894; Sloan Bruce, b. Dec. 17, 1897.

    8. JESSE DENDY STRIBLING, b. March 24, 1871; d. June 9, 1898; m. Jan. 31, 1894, *Sudie A. Buchannan:* issue,—Fred Dendy, b. Nov. 17, 1894; Neta, b. Oct. 19, 1897; d. April 27, 1898.

Note 1.   Taliaferro and Smith Families.

§87.   *Robert Taliaferro, Gent.*, the founder of this family in Virginia, and undoubtedly of English parentage, settled in Gloucester county in 1636 where he received a large grant of land.   He also owned extensive possessions in what is now Essex County.   He married a daughter of the Reverend Charles Grymes of Middlesex County, and had at least five sons,—Francis (m. Elizabeth Catlett), John (m. Sarah Smith), Richard, Charles, and Robert (m. Sarah Catlett).

John Taliaferro was born about 1660 and died in 1720, his will (made June 1, 1715) being probated in the Essex Court June 21, 1720.   About 1682 he married Sarah Smith, daughter of Col. Lawrence Smith of Gloucester county (see below).   On June 19, 1699 he gave bond as sheriff of Essex County, and in the same year represented his county in the House of Burgesses. That he was prominent in the early Colonial Wars with the Indians is shown by the record of Oct. 31, 1692, in the Calendar of Virginia State Papers, that "Lieut John Taliaferro gives return of his expenses in Tobacco, as Ranger with eleven men & two Indians", etc.   The records of York and Essex Counties show that his children were,—Lawrence, John, Charles, Robert, Zachariah, Richard, William, Mary, *Elizabeth* (who married THOMAS STRIBLING, §22), Sarah and Catherine.   It is this last named Robert Taliaferro of St. Paul's Parish, Stafford County, who, in his will dated Dec. 3, 1725 and recorded in the Essex Court June 21, 1726, mentions his sister Elizabeth, the wife of "Thomas Stripling", and her sons Francis, William and Taliaferro "Stripling".

Col. Lawrence Smith, of Abingdon Parish, Gloucester County, was a man of great influence and wealth in his day.   He bore the coat-of-arms of the Smiths of Tottne, County Devonshire, England, from which place he had perhaps emigrated to the Colony.   His wife's name was Mary ...., and his will was dated Aug. 8, 1700, but no copy of it has been preserved. He was surveyor for the counties of Gloucester and York in 1686, and in 1691 laid out the town of Yorktown.   In 1699 he was recommended by the Governor among the "gentlemen of estate and standing" suitable for appointment to the Council, but his death the following lyear 'prevented the bestowal of this honor upon him. He was conspicuous also as a leader in the early Colonial Wars. In 1676 he commanded "111 men out of Gloucester Co." at a fort near the falls of the Rappahannock River, and the same year he led the "trained bands" of Gloucester against the rebels under Bacon. The following were his children, as far as is known:—

1. John, of Gloucester County; member of the Council and county lieutenant.
2. Lawrence, of York County; Colonel, Justice, Sheriff of the County, and member of the House of Burgesses.
3. William.
4. Augustine, of St. Mary's Parish, Essex; one of the first bench of justices for Spotsylvania County in 1722.
5. Charles, of Essex County; died in 1710.
6. Elizabeth, m. Capt. John Battaile of St. Mary's Parish, Essex, and had issue: John, Lawrence, Hay, Nicholas, and others.
7. *Sarah Smith*, m. John Taliaferro, as above.

(See "Old King William Homes & Families", p. 101; Calendar of Virginia State Papers, Vol. I, p. 44; Stanard's "Colonial Virginia Register", p. 92; "William & Mary Quarterly", Vol. II, p. 5 and Vol. IX, p. 42.

Note 2. Tate Family.

§88 *Magnus Tate*, the first of the name in this country, emigrated from the Orkney Islands, north of Scotland, and landed at Philadelphia May 20, 1696, eventually locating in that part of Frederick County, Virginia, which finally became Jefferson County, West Virginia. He is said to have died in Sept. 1747. On May 2, 1749, Honour Tate, evidently his wife, qualified in the Frederick Court as administratrix of his estate. The inventory of his property was filed May 8, 1749. She must have died shortly afterwards, since it is recorded that on August 16, 1750 Magnus Tate qualified as administrator of Honour Tate, dec'd., and the inventory of her estate was filed Oct. 29, 1750. Their home was near Charlestown, now in Jefferson County, W. Va. As far as is known, they had only one child.

Magnus Tate, b. April 5, 1732; d. "Belvidere", in March 1808; m. Frederick County, Sept. 26, 1759. Mary Riley McCormick (b. in 1736; d. in 1810; see §193). They lived at "Belvidere", near Charlestown. which estate was perhaps the home of his father also. Their seven children were,—

A. Mary Tate, b. Feb 2, 1761; m. Joseph Daugherty: issue,— Ennis (d. in California), William (m. a Miss Henderson, but left no children), and Mary (never married).

B. *Ann* (usually called *Nancy*) *Tate*, b. Feb. 15, 1763; m. FRANCIS STRIBLING; see §24.

C. *Margaret* (usually called *Peggy*) *Tate*, b.in 1765; d in 1830; m. May 12, 1785, Battaile Muse (b. April 30, 1751; d. March 29, 1803; p. Col. George Muse and Elizabeth Battaile. Col. Muse was born in England in 1720 and was a Major in the English Army. He left the army about the same time as Lawrence Washington, and settled in Virginia. He achieved some distinction as Adjutant in the Spanish Wars, and wrote a book on military discipline. He is said to have instructed Washington in the evolution and movement of troops. In 1754 he was engaged in an expedition against the French and Indians, and also rendered conspicuous service in the Revolutionary War, for which he received a large grant of land in Kentucky, where he died in 1790. See Washington's "Life" by Weems, Irving, and Schroder. Battaile Muse was the attorney for General Washington in the management of his estate.)

I. George Augustine Muse. d. early unmarried.

II. Battaile Muse. d. early unmarried.

III. *Mary* (or *Polly*) *Muse*, m. Dr. John H. Lewis of Loudoun County.

    1. James B. Lewis, m. Ann Hume: issue,—Mary (d. unmarried), Robert (m. Cary Jones of Winchester: issue,—Rebecca, m. Rev. Charles N. Tyndall, and Annie),Virginia (m. John H. Kemp of Rockville, Md.; one son, James), Bettie (m. Charles H. Lewis: issue,— Virginia and Ann; see below), and Kate (unmarried).

    2. *Fisher Ames Lewis*, m. ELIZABETH LANE: no children; see §70.

    3. Charles H. Lewis. m. Estelle Green: issue,—Charles H. (m. his cousin Bettie Lewis; see above), John (m. Jessie Camden; several children), James (married and

lives in the West), Magnus M. (m. Susie Rose; three children; 1. Fredericksburg), Arthur (unmarried; is a minister in West Virginia), Gertrude (m. Minteo Ralston of Clarksburg, W. Va.; two children), Aldridge and George.

4. John H. Lewis, m. a Miss Kennedy of Maryland: issue,—Fisher Ames (1. Philadelphia, Pa.), Henry St. Pierre, and Ellen.

5. Mary Jane Lewis.

6. Dr. Magnus M. Lewis, m. Evelyn Brent of Alexandria; no children.

7. Joseph Newton Lewis, died in California, unmarried.

8. Robert Vincent Lewis, m. Belle Boyd of Kentucky; three sons.

9. *William Hierome Thomas Lewis*, m. *1st*. Belle S. Green of Falmouth; m. *2nd*. CATHERINE STUART NEILL; see §52. He had five children by the first marriage:—William Green (d. Nov. 7, 1900; m. Mary M. Beardsley of Kentucky; one daughter, Annabelle), Joseph Newton (m. Lyle O. Davidson of Selma, Ala.; no children), Duff Green (m. Agnes M. Proctor of England; no children), Alexander M. (m. Sallye Stone of Texas; one son, William Stone), and Ann Payne (unmarried).

IV. Elizabeth Battaile Muse, m. Jan. 4, 1810, Joseph Smith of Staunton. One child,

1. Elizabeth Smith, m. Robert S. Brooke: issue,—

(1). Margaret Brooke, m. Thomas P. Eskridge: issue,—Elizabeth (m. M. Filmore Gilkerson; three children, Janie, Eskridge and Maslin), Brooke (m. Nellie Garber; two sons), Meta (m. R. Spottswood Payne; two sons, Edwin and Robert), and Mary (m. James Anderson; one child).

(2). Virginia Brooke, m. Dr. Briscoe Baldwin Donaghe: issue,—Mary Berkeley (m. .... Mauzey; two children,—Catherine and Richard), Florence (m. Charles Hutcheson), Virginia (m. Matthew Fletcher; five children; 1. San Francisco) and George Price.

(3.) Elizabeth Brooke, m. Col. James C. Cochran
of "Folly": —issue, John, James, Anne Elizabeth (m. L. Seymour Rawlinson, son of the late
Canon George Rawlinson of Canterbury Cathe-
dral; one daughter, Elizabeth Seymour), Joseph
Smith (1. Staunton).

V. Margaret Muse, m. in May 1811, Major Hierome Lindsay Opie.

1. Hierome Lindsay Opie, m. Annie Locke of Martinsburg: issue,—Hierome Lindsay, Dr. Thomas of
Baltimore, May (m. Dr. Basil Meade), and Hon.
John N. Opie of Staunton (m. Ida Fletcher; see
below).

2. Juliet Opie, m. *1st.* Maj. Gordon; m. *2nd.* a Mr.
Hopkins, Member of Congress from Alabama. She
left no children.

3. Mary Opie, m. William Norris: issue,— William
and Wormley.

4. Virginia Opie, m. Robert Hume Butcher of Baltimore: issue,—Hume, Charles, Jennie, Juliet (m. Gen.
Ayres), Margaret and others.

5. Margaret Opie, m. Hon. George Reed Riddle, Senator from Delaware; she left no children.

VI. Magnus Tate Muse, died in August 1811, unmarried.

VII. Lucinda Muse, b. August 17, 1797; d. in Feb. 1859;
m. in 1816, Rev. William Claiborne Walton (d. Feb. 18,
1834).

1. Margaret Ann Walton, d. in 1825.

2. William Claiborne Walton, d. in 1837.

3. Lucy Muse Walton, b. May 3, 1822; m. in 1847,
Rev. Patterson Fletcher (d. in 1891).

(1). Lucinda Fletcher, d. in infancy.

(2). William Walton Fletcher, d. unmarried in
1895.

(3). Nannie Fletcher, m. in 1885, John W. Ba-
sore of Broadway.

(4). Minnie Fletcher, m. Rev. William A. Mackey, D. D., now of Whatcom, Washington State.

(5). Ida Fletcher, m. Hon. John N. Opie of
Staunton: see above.

(6). Lucy Fletcher, m. Mortimer Wilson Smith of Clarksburg, W. Va.

4. Eliza Walton, b. August 8, 1824; d. May 21, 1877; m. Alexandria, June 3, 1843, Rev. Rufus Wheelwright Clark of the Dutch Reformed Church, brother of Bishop Clark of the Episcopal Church.

(1). Rev. Rufus Wheelwright Clark, b. Portsmouth, N. H., May 29, 1844; m. April 9, 1874, Lucy Dennison, daughter of William Dennison, War-Governor of Ohio, and Postmaster General under President Lincoln: issue,—Helen (b. Jan. 18, 1875); Rufus Wheelwright (b. Dec. 20, 1876); Elizabeth (b. Feb. 27, 1879; m. Sept. 24,1901, Harry W. Leonard; one son, Raymond Clark, b. June 23,. 1902); William Dennison (b. Oct. 21, 1885); Jane Dennison (b. June 7, 1889). He is Rector of an Episcopal Church in Detroit, Mich.

(2). Rev. William Walton Clark, b. Portsmouth, N. H., May 8, 1846; m. March 4, 1868, Elizabeth M. Wyckoff of Brooklyn: issue,—Elizabeth Morris (b. December 8, 1869; now in Wellington, South Africa); Marion (b. May 15, 1875); Alice Webster (b. Nov. 11, 1877); l. Brooklyn, N. Y.

(3). Edward Warren Clark, b. Portsmouth, N.H., Jan. 27, 1849; m. Sept. 10, 1879, Louisa McCulloch: issue,—Edith Louisa (b. Sept. 2, 1880); Edward Warren (b. Feb. 17, 1882); Robert Stanton (b. March 16, 1884; d. Nov. 17, 1892); Henry McCulloch (b. Feb. 26, 1887); Robert Ernest (b. Jan. 10, 1889); Lucius Lehman (b. Jan. 26, 1891); Margery Williston (b. July 1, 1896); l. Tallahassee, Fla.

(4). Rev. Fletcher Clark, b. Boston, Mass., Nov. 23, 1852; m. Nov. 7, 1881, Elizabeth Matson Nyce; one daughter, Lillian Matson (b. Nov. 26, 1884); l. Philadelphia, Penn.

(5). Francke Lucien Clark, b. Brooklyn, N. Y., April 15, 1859; l. Philadelphia, Penn., unmarried.

(6). Eliza Walton Clark, b. Albany, N. Y., Aug. 27, 1865; m. Sept. 19, 1888, Theodore H. Eaton: issue,—Theodore Horatio (b. June 23, 1889; d. in 1891); Margaret Montgomery (b. May 9, 1892); Berrien Clark (b. August 3, 1893); l. Detroit, Mich.

5. Henry Martyn Walton, d. in 1877; m. Magdalene Neill of Jefferson County, W. Va.; one child, Lily, widow of Ruthven Morrow of Charlestown, W. Va.

6. Rev. Edward Payson Walton, m. Janet Skinker of Richmond: issue,—Rev. William (Archdeacon of Georgia), May and Edward.

7. Rev. Jeremiah Evarts Walton, b. March 27, 1831; m. Helen Mar Randal of Massachusetts: issue,— William, Helen (m. her cousin, Rev. W. W. Walton), Lucy (m. Hyde Marshall Mich), Jeremiah, Florence (m. Charles Gorham), Marshall Mich.

8. Rev. Robert Hall Walton, m. Annie Lewis of Harrisonburg: issue,—Maude (m............ Mays of Birmingham, Ala.), Minnie, Rev. Fletcher (a minister of the Methodist Church in Georgia), William, Robert (of Atlanta, Ga.), Francke.

§89 D. *Magnus Tate*, b. "Belvidere", Sept. 1, 1767; d. March 30, 1823; m. Mrs. Elizabeth Tryatt–Shrodes (p. John Tryatt and Elizabeth Tillottson, great-grand-daughter of the Archbishop of Canterbury; they were very wealthy, and came to America about 1770). He was elected to the Virginia House of Representatives in 1797, '98, '99, 1802, '03, '09, and '10. He was commissioned Magistrate in 1799, and was twice commissioned Sheriff of the County, in 1819 and 1820. In 1815 he was elected to the United States Congress. He was a Trustee of Charlestown at its establishment in 1786. His home was about three miles from Martinsburg.

I. Erasmus Tate, m. Ann Packett of Charlestown. He died at the age of seventy-five, leaving no children.

II. John Tate.

III. *Mary Tate*, m. DR. TALIAFERRO STRIBLING; see §33.

IV. Lucinda Tate, m. George Thomas of Hancock, Md.; two sons, Erasmus of Springfield, Ohio, and James.

V. Amanda (?) Tate, perhaps married a Mr. Goode.

E. John Tate, died unmarried.

F. George Tate, died unmarried.

§90 G. William Tate, b. "Belvidere", Jan. 20, 1776; d. in 1818; m. Feb. 5, 1807, Abigail North Humphreys (b. July 4, 1787; d. Nov. 15, 1862; p. David Humphreys, immigrant from Wales, and Ann North, daughter of Roger North and Ann Rambo, and grand-daughter of Caleb North, who landed in Philadelphia, from Cork, Ireland, July 20, 1729).

 I. Mary Ann Tate, b. in 1808; d. Jan. 22, 1832; m. a Mr. Daugherty: issue,—Mary A. (d. unmarried in 1888), W. T., and others.

 II. Dr. Magnus W. Tate of Lexington, Mo., married twice: issue, by second marriage,—Gay, John, William, a daughter who married George Crawford of Louisville, Ky., and others.

 III. Willelma Tate, b. in 1813; d. Sept. 20, 1853; m. a Mr. Aisquith of Baltimore, Md.; issue,—Mary V., Lyttleton, William, and others.

 IV. George H. Tate, d. unmarried in Cincinnati, Ohio, April 25, 1890.

 V. John Humphreys Tate, b. "Belvidere", Dec. 26, 1816; d. Feb. 7, 1891; m. Cincinnati, O., May 11, 1853, Margaret Kincaid Chenoweth (b. Harrodsburg, Ky., Jan. 8, 1832; d. Feb. 2, 1889).

    1. John Chenoweth Tate, b. Cincinnati, O., March 11, 1854; m. in Oct. 1876, Fanny Casey: issue,—James Casey, Margaret Chenoweth, and John H.; l. Kansas City, Mo.

    2. Abbie Humphreys Tate, b. Cincinnati, O., Feb. 8, 1856; m. Perrin G. March; l. Fernbank, O.: issue,— Margaret Churchward (b. April 2, 1882); Janet Louise (b. August 10, 1886); Perrin Flack (b. July 26, 1888).

    3. William Ross Tate, b. Cincinnati, O., Feb. 14, 1858; l. Chicago, Ill.

    4. Lizzie Polk Tate, b. Cincinnati, O., Dec. 14, 1860; d. ib. Sept. 2, 1867.

    5. George North Tate, b. ib. March 22, 1863; l. Chicago, Ill.

    6. Thomas Orkney Tate, b. Cincinnati, O., June 17, 1865; l. ib.

    7. Dr. Magnus Alfred Tate, b. ib. Nov. 12, 1867; m. Nov. 25, 1896, Katherine Welch Donnally; l. ib.

(1). Miriam Welch Tate, b. May 1, 1898.
8. Frank McCormick Tate, b. ib. Dec. 18, 1869; d. ib. Jan. 30, 1871.
9. Ralph Booth Tate, b. ib. Oct. 10, 1872; l. ib.

Note 3. Snickers Family.

§91. *Edward Snickers* was a wealthy planter and large land owner of Frederick County. A town in Loudoun County, a gap in the Blue Ridge, and a ferry on the Shenandoah all took their name from him. He died late in 1790. About 1755 he is said to have married Elizabeth Taliaferro, perhaps a niece of the Elizabeth Taliaferro who married the first Thomas Stribling (see §§22 and 23), and had four children. No descendants by the name of Snickers remain today.

A. *Sarah Snickers*, b. June 18, 1756; m. Feb. 12, 1773, Morgan Alexander (b. Jan. 10, 1746); she had one child,

I. *Elizabeth Alexander*, m. Nov. 10, 1796, James Ware (b. July 13, 1771; p. James Ware and Catherine Todd). Three children,—

1. *Sarah Elizabeth Taliaferro Ware*, m. SIGISMUND STRIBLING; see §45.

2. Charles Alexander Ware.

3. Josiah William Ware, b. August 7, 1802; d. August 13, 1883; m. *1st.* Feb. 22, 1827, Frances Toy Glassell; m. *2nd.* Edmonia Jaquelin Smith (see below, §92). There were six children by the first marriage and four by the second.

(1). James Ware.

(2). Hon. James Alexander Ware, m. Jane Morton Smith: issue,—Fannie (m. ....Elliott), Summerville, Eudora (m. ....Deane).

(3). John Glassell Ware.

(4). Elizabeth Alexander Ware, m. *1st.* Dr. Edward Wharton Britton, and had one son, Josiah Ware Britton; m. *2nd.* Dr. James Mercer Garnet McGuire; l. Berryville.

(5). Lucy Balmain Ware, m. Edward Parke Custis Lewis: issue,—Eleanor Angela, Lawrence

Fielding, John Glassell, Edward Parke Custis, Lucy Ware (m. Charles McCormick of Chicago).

(6). Charles Alexander Ware; 1. St. Louis, Mo.

(7). Jaquelin Smith Ware, m. Helen Grinnan; 1. Clarke County.

(8). Rev. Sigismund Stribling Ware, m. Elizabeth Walker: issue,—Cornelia, Edmonia Jaquelin, Edward Jaquelin; he is Rector of the Episcopal Church at Port Royal.

(9). Rev. Josiah William Ware, m. Annie Nottingham: issue,—Helen, John Nottingham, Jaquelin, Josiah William, Kennard; he is Rector of the Episcopal Church at Ashland.

(10). Robert Mackey Ware, m. Caroline Waughop: issue,—Ellen, Josiah William, Harry, Alice Wilson; 1. Chicago, Ill.

B. *Catherine Snickers*, b. August 20, 1757, m. Dr Robert Mackey of Winchester.

   I. Mary Mackey, m. Samuel Taylor.

     1. Mary Taylor, m. Dr. R. McKim Holliday.

       (1). Mary Holliday, m. Thomas McCormick of "Elmington", as his third wife; see §200.

       (2). Col. Frederick William Mackey Holliday, m. *1st*. Hannah McCormick (see §200); m. *2nd*. Caroline Stuart. He was elected Governor of Virginia in 1877.

       (3). Margaret Holliday, m. Dr. G. F. Mason: issue,—Mary Herbert Mason; 1. Charlestown, W. Va.

       (4). Dr. Samuel Taylor Holliday.

     2. Robert Mackey Taylor.

     3. Charles Taylor.

     4. Elizabeth Taylor.

§92 II. Betsy Mackey, m. Edward Jaquelin Smith of "Smithfield", Clarke County.

     1. Catharine V. Smith, m. Edward Hall: issue,—Emily, Virginia, Betty Mackey, Adelaide (m. Roger Annan).

     2. *William Dickerson Smith*, m. *1st*. MARGARET FRANCES STRIBLING (see §31); m. *2nd*. Agnes Williams: issue by second marriage.

(1). Rev. William Dickerson Smith, m. Lucy Harrison Powers: issue,—Agnes Pickett, Annie Jaquelin, William Dickerson, Mary Bryson; he is Rector of St. George's Episcopal Church at Fredericksburg.

(2). Edward Jaquelin Smith, m. Mary Thompson: issue,– Lucile Pickett, Mary Jaquelin; 1. Wickliffe.

(3). Annie Williams Smith, m. Richard Buckner Smith; 1. Wickliffe.

(4). Elizabeth Mackey Smith, m. Robert Randolph Smith: issue,—Elizabeth Mackey, Agnes Williams, Susie Wellford; 1. Wickliffe.

3. Edmonia J. Smith, m. Josiah William Ware; see above, §91.

4. Edward Smith.

5. Elizabeth Bush Smith, m. *1st.* John Bush; m. *2nd.* Oliver Tousey. There were three children by the first marriage and four by the second.

(1). Catherine Bush.

(2). Mary Bush.

(3). Betty Bush.

(4). Olive Tousey, m. F. A. Fletcher: issue,—Bessie, Frank, Roberta, Catherine; 1. Evanston, Ill.

(5). Emily Tousey, m. Truston B. Boyd: issue,—David, Ingram; 1. St. Louis, Mo.

(6). Lydia Paxton Tousey, m. George W. Boyd, Asst. Genl. Pass. Agent of the Pennsylvania R. R.: issue,—Oliver, Lydia Paxton, Anna; 1. Philadelphia, Penn.

(7). Roberta Tousey, m. Stanley Grepe: issue,—John Stanley, Lydia Jaquelin; 1. Evanston, Ill.

6. Emily Smith.

7. Roberta Mackey Smith, m. Philip Powers; 1. Wickliffe.

(1). Alice Burnett Powers.

(2). Elizabeth Mackey Powers.

(3). Jaquelin Smith Powers, m. Estelle Castleman: issue,—Roberta, Mary, Estelle, Emily, Henry, Fannie Catherine, Sophie.

(4). William Smith Powers, m. Jeanette Brown: issue,—Jeanette; 1. Chicago, Ill.

(5). Fannie Ballard Powers, m. Rev. T.Carter Page: issue,—Philip Powers, Virginia Newton, Roberta Mackey; 1. Cambridge, Md.

(6). Kate Stuart Powers.

(7). Philip H. Powers, m. Mary Grove: issue,—Philip H., Louise Berry; 1. Clarke County.

(8). Mary H. Powers.

(9). Edmonia Ware Powers.

III. Frederick Mackey.

IV. John Mackey, m. Rebecca McGuire.

    1. Frederika Mackey, m. Nathan S. White of Jefferson County.

        (1). Benjamin White.

        (2). Rebecca White. m. Joseph Trapnell: issue,—Benjamin, Emily, Joseph, Frederika, Ellen, William, White, Rebecca, Thomas, Richard, John Mackey; 1. Charlestown, W. Va.

    2. Elizabeth Mackey, m. John Meade.

        (1). Catherine Meade, m. James William Fletcher: issue,—William Meade, James; 1. Rappahannock County.

        (2). Louise Meade, m..........Richie.

        (3). Mary Meade.

        (4). John Meade.

    3. Catherine Mackey, m. Scott Tidball.

        (1). Nannie Tidball, m..........Dickinson: issue,—Warren, Catherine.

        (2). Rev. Thomas A. Tidball, D. D., m. Josephine Brown; 1. Philadelphia, Pa.

V. Sally Mackey, m. Dr. Robert T. Baldwin; no issue.

§93 VI. *Kitty Mackey*, m. Dr. Archibald Stuart Baldwin.

    1. Mary Mackey Baldwin, m. Joseph Tidball, a lawyer.

        (1). Stuart Baldwin Tidball.

        (2). William Hill Tidball, m. Mary Swartzwelder: issue,—Leonard; 1. Fort Worth, Texas.

        (3). Susan Watkins Tidball, m. E. M. Tidball; 1. Winchester.

The following was omitted by mistake from the opposite page.

> **4½.** Dr. Robert Frederick Baldwin, m. Caroline Marx Barton. He was a Colonel and Surgeon in the Confederate Army, and Superintendent of the Western State Hospital for the Insane at Staunton.
>
> > (1). Caroline Marx Baldwin, m. Hugh Caperton Preston: issue,—James Francis, Robert Baldwin, Caroline Marx, Sarah Caperton, William Ballard and Katherine Stuart.
> >
> > (2). Katherine Mackey Baldwin, m. Barton Myers of Norfolk: issue,—Robert Baldwin, Julia Barton, Katherine Barton, Louisa Barton, Caroline Barton, Barton, and Frances Stuart.
> >
> > (3). Archibald Stuart Baldwin, m. Martha Frazier; issue,—Robert Frederick, Martha Frazier, Archibald Stuart, William Frazier, Caroline Barton, Howard Frazier and Katherine Mackey.
> >
> > (4). Robert Frederick Baldwin, m. Elizabeth Deans Boykin: issue,—Robert Frederick, Elizabeth Irwin and William Boykin.
> >
> > (5). William Barton Baldwin, m. Bessie Saunders Taylor: no issue.
> >
> > (6). John Mackey Baldwin, unmarried.

      (4). Robert Baldwin Tidball.

      (5). Catherine Stuart Tidball.

  2. Margaret Daniel Baldwin, m. Robert Whitehead, a lawyer.

      (1). Stuart Baldwin Whitehead, m. Susan Massay: issue,—John, Stuart Baldwin, Robert, Katherine; 1. Lovingston, Nelson County.

      (2). Kittie Mackey Whitehead, m. Frederick Moss: issue,—Kimbrough, Jean Irwin, Margaret, Archibald Stuart Baldwin; 1. Markham.

      (3). Mary Briscoe Whitehead.

      (4). Samuel Whitehead.

      (5). Sarah Whitehead.

      (6). Robert Frederick Whitehead.

  3. *Catherine Snickers Baldwin*, m. DR. SIGISMUND STRIBLING NEILL; see §51.

  4. Sarah Elizabeth Taliaferro Baldwin.

  5. *Dr. John Mackey Baldwin*, m. Martha W. Barton.

      (1). Archibald Stuart Baldwin, m. Emma Clark: issue,—Laura, Mildred.

      (2). *Maria Marshall Baldwin*, m. JAMES RICHARDS TAYLOR; see §11.

  6. Dr. Cornelius Baldwin, m. Anna Marshall Jones:

      (1). Charles Marshall Baldwin, m. Belle Hammat.

  7. Fannie Ware Baldwin.

C. William Snickers, b. in July, 1759; m. May 30, 1793, Frances Washington, daughter of Warner and Mary (Whiting) Washington.

  I. Mary Snickers, m. Moses Hunter: issue,—Frances Washington, Nancy (m. William Weeks; issue,—Mary, Fannie, William, Brooke. Hunter; 1. Washington, D. C.), Moses, Henry St. George, Beverley, and Brooke.

  II. Emily Snickers.

  III. Betty Snickers, m. Henry Brown: issue,—Frederick, William, Frank, Fannie, and others.

  IV. William Snickers.

  V. Beverley Snickers.

  VI. Edward Snickers.

D. *Elizabeth Snickers*, m. THOMAS STRIBLING, see §63.

www.ingramcontent.com/pod-product-compliance
Lightning Source LLC
Chambersburg PA
CBHW030516100426
42813CB00001B/58